MW01289712

Ancient China

A Captivating Guide to the Ancient History of China and the Chinese Civilization Starting from the Shang Dynasty to the Fall of the Han Dynasty

Free Bonus from Captivating History (Available for a Limited time)

Hi History Lovers!

Now you have a chance to join our exclusive history list so you can get your first history ebook for free as well as discounts and a potential to get more history books for free! Simply visit the link below to join.

Captivatinghistory.com/ebook

Also, make sure to follow us on Facebook, Twitter and Youtube by searching for Captivating History.

Contents

Introduction

China today is a country of many controversies. Its industry is booming, but it's a socialist state. The communist party is the undisputed ruler of the entire nation, with many Orwellian features in its dictatorship. Even Chinese society seems to be rather collectivistic in nature. With the centralized economy, a strong people's army, and a clear leftist ideology, China today is without a doubt a communist country, which, unlike most of its predecessors, seems to be functioning and here to stay. But despite all that, there is a resemblance between this modern People's Republic and Imperial China of the past, as the same blood of the red dragon flows through its veins. And though ideology has changed quite substantially, it looks like the philosophy behind it remained the same. So, to understand present-day China, its politics, society, and culture in general, we have to go back to the beginnings of the Chinese civilization.

It was during this early period that the Chinese people emerged from a local power to one of the most important states in the world, developing its own worldviews, philosophy of life and politics, and creating a civilization to last millennia to come. And no matter how much time has passed, and the influence that came through time, these roots remain deeply embedded in Chinese society. The best examples of this are the thoughts of Confucius as well as the writings of Sun Tzu, both of whom lived in during the period of ancient China; these two figures are probably the most well-known Chinese in the world, rivaled only by the infamous chairman Mao. But even if you are not curious about understanding how China came to be today, you should be interested in Chinese history, as some of the world's greatest achievements in science, technology, philosophy, and art came from its civilization. Its contribution to the cultural heritage of the human race is enormous; one may even argue the most important. Yet due to misunderstandings and current political climate, Western audiences often overlook it. And that is a mistake that should not be made.

And this guide is a good first step in avoiding that mistake. You will be led on a journey through almost 2,000 years of Chinese history, showing you all the ups and downs of those ancient times, the sufferings and joys of the Chinese people, along with their greatest achievements and failures. Dynasties will change, people will be killed and born, art made and destroyed, but the Chinese civilization will prevail, rising from humble beginnings to an empire that at some points outshined any other in the world at that time. And yet it won't be only a tale of kings and queens, emperors and rulers, of palaces and forts, or of swords and shields. It will also tell a story of farmers and merchants, artisans and artists, philosophers and scientists. And hopefully by the end of this introductory guide, you will gain a sense of what, who, and how the Chinese civilization was made as great as it was and still is. From that, a better understanding of this amazing Far Eastern culture and its history should arise as well as a greater appreciation of its achievements and contributions to the world. And with a better knowledge of history, a clearer understanding of the world will come as well.

Chapter 1 – Chinese Lands and Birth of China

A long, long time ago, a giant god named Pangu had awoken from a prolonged slumber in a chaotic egg-like shaped universe, finding only darkness around him. Unsatisfied, he used his ax to split the egg into two pieces creating the earth (black Yin) and the sky (white Yang). And after eighteen thousand years of loneliness, he died, leaving his body to decay and transform into mountains, rivers, forests, and other geological and botanical features. In one version, he created humans from clay before he died because he felt the universe was too empty, while in another they came from the fleas that lived on Pangu's fur, which were spread across the earth by the wind when he died. This is one of the old Chinese creation myths of both the universe and the human race, or to be more precise, the Chinese people. For centuries this was one of the stories in which the ancient Chinese believed in, but of course today, we know better than to look at the legends as the truth.

1. Illustration of giant god Pangu. Source: https://commons.wikimedia.org

Archeological facts give us a completely different story of the early settlement of China, which maybe isn't as imaginative or fun, but is by no mean less impressive. The oldest fossil remains found in China date around 2 million years ago. These remains are from Homo Erectus, the predecessor of Homo Sapiens, or modern man. This means that China was settled from the Early Stone Age, scientifically known as the Paleolithic Era. These pre-humans, as we might call the Homo Erectus, settled across large areas of what is modern China, and show rather significant diversity in their tool usage and way of life. Around 300,000 years ago, these pre-humans started to evolve into Homo Sapiens both in Africa, the cradle of humankind, as well as in Asia. Some of the earliest settlements of modern man in China dates from around 200-250,000 years ago, and from that time, development of tools and social life started to speed up until it culminated in what is today called the "Neolithic (New Stone Age) Revolution" that started somewhere between 8-10,000 years ago. In that period, agriculture developed in China, like in the other "cradles of civilization." The main crops of these Neolithic settlements were rice and millet. They also started to show signs of more complicated tools, like spears, arrows, hooks, and needles, as well as the first signs of rituals. These early cultures also domesticated dogs and pigs, and in later periods started making crude ceramics. Of course, it is too early to mark these early humans as the Chinese people, but they were most likely their ancestors.

The main area of the early settlements of the Chinese ancestors was around the Yellow (Huang) River and its largest tributary, Wei River, which lay south of present-day Beijing. Later on, they spread farther south to another major river in China, the Yangtze River, which is also the longest river in Asia. These areas weren't chosen randomly, but thanks to the flooding and the fertilizing materials they brought from the plains on the east, they made a rather fertile land on their banks. That made them rather attractive for the early humans as they made farming much easier with their primitive tools. Another important detail is the fact that roughly in the middle between the Yellow and Yangtze Rivers draws the line where rice cultivation stops due to the change in the climate. The warmer and rainier weather to the south of that line allows for rice to be grown, and also makes southern China more tropical, with dense jungles and heavy rainfalls. On the north, millet was the main crop as the climate is more continental, with mild and warm summers and rather cold winters. And also, there is much less rain in northern China. It is also worth noting that the area between these two major rivers is mostly flat, with mountains growing taller as you head west. On the northwestern borders of these plains lies a dry steppe which eventually turns into a desert today known as the Gobi, near the modern Chinese-Mongolian border. In the east and south lies the Yellow Sea and the Pacific Ocean, in which both of the aforementioned rivers flow into.

Even from the basic geography, two things become obvious rather quickly. First, the land between the Yellow and Yangtze Rivers is rather fertile and suitable for settlement. That is apparent from the fact that even today the most densely populated area of China is the region between those rivers. The other is that the lands of the early

Chinese were surrounded by natural obstacles: thick jungles to the south, high mountains to the west, dry deserts to the north, and a vast ocean to the east. This allowed the early Chinese society to grow separately from the other people and cultures that were around them, allowing for a rather unique and specific development of the Chinese civilization. By the early 3rd millennia BCE, various local cultures that sprang up between the two major rivers started to slowly merge into one melting pot through trade, warfare, and other contacts. Their societies became more complex, with a ruling class on top, together with kings and shamans, and the working class on the bottom, mainly farmers. The first cities in the Chinese heartland were created, and around that time, China entered the Copper Age, abandoning stone for more advanced metal tools and weapons, which was a transition from the Neolithic to the Bronze Age. This was the beginning of what could be called proto-Chinese civilization.

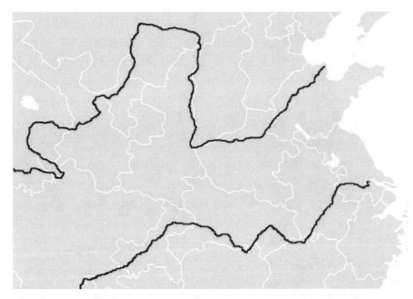

2. Map of central China with marked Yellow and Yangtze Rivers with modern provinces. Source: https://commons.wikimedia.org

Unfortunately for historians, the entire 3rd millennia BCE is shrouded by the numerous myths and legends that were written down in the later generations, and with only limited archeological findings, it is rather difficult to piece the exact events. Stories written down by early Chinese historians, like Sima Qian, tell us that in the early days the Three Sovereigns ruled one after another after the death of Pangu, and they were credited with creating order in the newly formed universe. They supposedly separated humans into tribes, gave them suitable rulers, organized the moving of the sun and the moon, and divided China into nine traditional provinces. These were some of the many feats attributed to them. These earliest rulers were seen as semi-divine, living for many thousands of years, having supernatural features, strength, and other inhuman characteristics. After them came the Five Emperors, starting with the Yellow Emperor. Traditionally his rule is dated to somewhere between 2700 and 2600 BCE, and he was often seen as the father of the Chinese people. He was the first who gave an order to the life of humans, teaching his nomadic brethren how to build shelters, farm, tame animals, and make clothes. He even gave them their first laws, the first version of the modern Chinese calendar, and taught them early math and writing. In essence, the myths tell us that he had created the Chinese civilization.

3. Ancient drawing depicting the Yellow Emperor. Source:
  https://commons.wikimedia.org

But as he was a mere human, he died after reaching 113 years of life, leaving the throne to the next emperor. The next four emperors also ruled for a long time, most of them also managing to celebrate over 100 birthdays. And all of them were also very wise, capable rulers who further developed and bettered the life of the people. They brought music, art, and games (such as the traditional board game Weiqi, or Go), as well as regulated the social system into a patriarchal feudalism, forbade inter-kin marriage, and organized early religion. All of them also supposedly gave up their thrones willingly to the people they deemed more virtuous and worthier to rule. And interestingly the successors they chose were usually not from their families. The last emperor, Shun, gave his throne to Yu, today known as Yu the Great, who was a proven hero who managed to subdue the floods that troubled China at the time by building canals and dams, essentially creating the irrigation systems. As such, he was seen as a perfect man to continue the enlightened rule of the previous emperors aiming to further develop China. Traditionally his rule is dated somewhere between around 2200 and 2100 BCE, and he was seen as the ideal ruler, a wise philosopher king, who managed to unite various tribes, impose fair taxes, build roads, and distribute food, making China under his rule a land of overall welfare.

These stories of great mythical emperors are easily dismissible as pure fiction that was created in later centuries when they were written down, especially considering no concrete evidence of their rule has been found yet. No records remain, no tombs have been excavated, and not even a monument of some sort dating from their era has been uncovered. And for a long time, they have been dismissed by historians as nothing more than legends. But with new archeological findings, their interpretations have changed. Now they think these myths were actually based in reality in some aspects. During the 3rd millennia, Chinese civilization did go through its forming period, achieving almost all of the aforementioned feats of the great emperors. Their society started its stratification, where slowly a ruling class started to emerge; shamans and religion had been formed; they created their own calendar; and they showed early signs of writing, though they had not yet fully developed a writing system. Villages built irrigation systems allowing for better yields of crops which could withstand a larger population, leading to the growth of larger societies. Also, roads and early transportation devices like chariots and boats were built, which led to a tighter connection between different tribes and villages. The ceramics were now more delicate, with nicer decorations, while jade ware, now synonymous with Chinese classical art, have been found in tombs. This shows that the leap in the division of labor had been made at this time as this shows that there were artisans focused solely on their crafts.

Yet despite all those developments depicted in the stories, historians deduced that the society still hadn't moved on from the egalitarian clan system, where every member of the community was more or less equal to one another both in wealth and in position, precisely because in the stories mythical emperors weren't succeeded by their kids. They think that the ruling class still wasn't strong enough to enforce the hereditary rule, as most things, like land and cattle, were still shared among the tribe folk. But that separation did start during the 3rd millennia BCE, and according to the traditional Chinese chronology, it culminated around 2070 BCE when the last great emperor Yu left his throne to his son Qi. This leads historians to conclude that around that era a clear separation between the tribal elite, with a ruler at its head, and the commoners was achieved, leading China into the monarchical system. This moment also marks the birth of the first Chinese dynasty called Xia, starting the common division of Chinese history based on the ruling family. But even the historicity of the Xia has been questioned by many historians, as for a long time there was no direct evidence for their existence. Yet in the past several decades, new findings in the region where they supposedly ruled have shown that there was indeed a strong culture or a state that ruled over the lands mentioned in the myths, but no markings have been found clearly stating it was the Xia Dynasty.

4. Medieval painting of King Yu. Source: https://commons.wikimedia.org

Archeologists have found various vases, figurines, and other craftworks that indicate a rather sophisticated culture existed around the Yellow River at the beginning of the 2nd millennia BCE, along with new tools and weapons made out of bronze, clearly marking a point when China entered the Bronze Age. Also, some larger building projects, like royal palaces, have been unearthed in recent archeological surveys, with some historians suggesting that one of these sites may have been a Xia Dynasty capital. Now, these facts show us that roughly 4,000 years ago China lost the marks of the egalitarian tribal society completely. The ruling class became wealthy and powerful enough to command the commoners to build palaces, temples, or any other type of public works. Also, new technologies were adopted, most notably the casting of bronze, showing a rather important advance of the Chinese civilization. That combined with a more precise calendar allowed this supposed Xia culture to achieve a leap in farming production. And bronze weapons found clearly show that warfare became a more common thing among the ancient Chinese, which is also important for the social structure of the society, as the elites were tasked with the defense of the common population. But offensive wars also brought extra gains for the ruling class, further elevating them from the farmers and craftsmen.

Going back to the traditional sources, they tell us pretty much the same thing. Xia kings built palaces, waged wars with surrounding tribes, and expanded their territories, with a clear distinction developing between the rulers and elites from the commoners. These sources say that the Xia roughly ruled for 450 years. Their kings had their ups and downs, some being capable rulers, while others were either weak or abusive. But in the end, the entire dynasty has been held in high regard by the Chinese people throughout the centuries, with most of their rulers seen as the founding fathers of China. Their rule ended around 1600 BCE when one of the Xia vassals rebelled and overthrew Jie, the last Xia ruler, who was depicted as an abusive and poor ruler. That rebellious subject was Tang, the founder of the second Chinese dynasty called Shang. Today, the Xia Dynasty is still a controversial topic in Chinese history as some historians still see it as pure myth. A new theory has been proposed which states that the Xia did exist, but that they didn't actually rule over the entirety of China. Proponents of this theory point out that it is likely that later historians attributed that position to them, as in fact, the Xia state was the most powerful at the time, and its achievements were the best choice for historians to describe that period. In fact, they point out that according to the legends, the Shang and Zhou, the dynasties that came after the Xia, existed during the rule of that first dynasty.

In the end, choosing to believe in the stories of the Five Emperors or the Xia Dynasty isn't what is exactly important here. It is the fact that during the period described through these myths Chinese civilization was forged and formed into what we know today. These legends only tell us how the ancient Chinese themselves saw this transition through mythical and semi-mythical figures that led them from being wandering hunter-gatherers with stone tools to fully functional states and societies, armed with bronze and living in lavish palaces. And the ancient Chinese people have celebrated achievements of these long-gone ancestors, giving them due credit for all later accomplishments of Chinese culture. Finally, both these stories and the archeological evidence tell us one very important thing—how China was born.

Chapter 2 – Shang and Zhou Dynasties and the Rise of Royal Power

By the end of the 17th century BCE, the first Chinese dynasty had fallen and a new one had risen. The Shang Dynasty is the first historically confirmed dynasty that historians can clearly identify. It was also located in the basin of the Yellow River, continuing traditions and development of the Xia that came before them. And if the Xia did indeed build the foundations of Chinese civilization, the Shang were the ones that actually built it into what it is today. Under their reign, the imperial reign was solidified, further advances with bronze making and building were achieved, the calendar was further improved, and the writing system had been fully organized. And indeed, it is during the Shang Dynasty that China had gone from the prehistoric age to the age of recorded history, quickly rising from its humble beginnings into a civilization that could match any of its contemporaries.

That rise came with Tang, the first ruler of the Shang Dynasty, who at first was only a local subordinate of the Xia. Traditional histories tell us that he slowly gathered power and influence over the decades, mostly at the cost of the other Xia vassals. Slowly one by one, surrounding petty kingdoms, cities, and tribes fell under his rule, all while his suzerain, his feudal overlord, cared little. On the other hand, people and states that Tang conquered put up little resistance as Jie, the last Xia ruler, was a rather tyrannical king that cared little about his subordinates. Eventually, Tang's power grew and Jie's diminished, so the former vassal raised up against his superior and challenged his rule. When the battle was about to start, Tang gave a speech to his enemies, pointing out all of Jie's flaws, and according to tradition, many of the generals switched sides while common soldiers simply fled the battlefield. The Shang were victorious, and Jie had to run away, abandoning his throne. He spent the remaining years of his life in a monastery. And the new Shang Dynasty came to the throne. The exact year of this event is unknown; traditional history tells us it happened in the early 17th century, around 1675 BCE. But modern archeological surveys and in-depth analysis of the early Chinese histories indicate that it is more likely this happened somewhere around 1600.

The new Chinese ruler kept his word, and he first lowered taxes and reduced conscription for the royal army, making him more popular among the people. But despite the smaller army, Tang managed to widen his influence to surrounding tribes, actually increasing the size of the Shang state, ruling over the middle and lower Yellow River basin. And when the droughts burdened his people, he gave them money from his treasury to help them get by. For all of this, he is remembered as one of the best ancient Chinese kings. Yet regardless of this great start, it seems the early Shang Dynasty lacked stability as in the next 250 years their rulers changed the location of their capitals 5 times. Historians can't say why this happened, but it's most likely that the Shang rule wasn't secure and that they had to deal with many local and possibly external threats, so their rulers moved their capital across the country to either better deal with those problems or to establish their courts in more secure locations. But it seems that around 1350 BCE, Shang rulers managed to overcome these difficulties as King Pan Geng moved the Shang capital for the last time. He chose to return it to original capital of Tang, a location today called Anyang. This marked the start of the Shang golden age.

5. Map showing the territory of Shang Dynasty. Source: https://commons.wikimedia.org

That golden age was marked by peace, prosperity, and an overall rise in the might of the Shang state, achieved while Pan Geng was still alive. Some of the later Chinese records even tell us that he brought back some of Tang's reforms, both to appease his subjects and to restore his kingdom to its previous glory. After Pan's death, he was succeeded by his two younger brothers before his nephew, Wu Ding, came to the throne, under whose rule the Shang achieved their greatest success. His reign has been more precisely dated by modern historians, and it lasted for an astonishing 58 years from 1250 to 1192 BCE. He was both a capable diplomat and a great military commander. He managed to establish and reinforce alliances with many surrounding tribes by marrying one of the princesses from each tribe, making all of them his concubines. And those tribes which were too hostile and warmongering Wu Ding pacified and conquered through war. He conquered three neighboring tribes, while another two after seeing his might chose to send emissaries and negotiate for peace, fearing they might be next. Of course, that kind of power also meant that economically the Shang state flourished, both from trade and from a rise in quantity and quality of production of all sorts.

Astonishing advances achieved by the golden era Shang Dynasty can be corroborated by archeological evidence as well. In royal tombs of this period, hundreds of finely made bronze items like wine cups, chalices, religious vessels, weapons, and even chariot decorations have been discovered. Beside those various items made out of bronze, ivory and other more luxurious materials were found. Such rich findings certainly show how wealthy the elite had become at the height of Shang power. But more important were the quantities of bronze found in these tombs, some measuring in tons, which show how developed Chinese metallurgy had become. No other ancient civilization has produced as much bronze as Shang China did. That leads historians to believe that from the small-scale bronze production of the Xia era, China managed to develop large-scale production by 15th century BCE, creating something that in modern terms we would call proto-industry. Agriculture was booming as well, with sources mentioning that Shang rulers were draining lowland swampy fields and clearing wild vegetation from fertile lands. This meant that food production was rising as well, explaining how the last Shang capital managed to boast a population of an estimated 140,000 people in its heyday.

6. Shang period bronze tripod. Source: https://commons.wikimedia.org

Another sign of prosperity of the Shang state, or at least of its ruling elite, was the number of animal offerings in the temples. Usually, about ten head of cattle would be sacrificed, but for special occasions, these numbers would rise into the hundreds. And cattle weren't the only animals sacrificed. Ancient Chinese offered sheep, pigs, and even dogs to their gods. Of course, most of these animals and the pastures they fed upon were in the hands of the royal family and the elite, and it is highly unlikely that the commoners enjoyed as much meat as their rulers did.

But despite how important the development of large-scale animal husbandry was to the Chinese civilization, it could be argued that the introduction of horses and chariots was more important. Current evidence suggests that this important advancement happened in the 13th century, most likely through the nomadic tribes that lived in the Central Asian steppes, as the domestication of horses first occurred in the Caucasus and the Middle East. Domestication and use of horses were important advances that made travel easier and faster, and they were also useful as work animals and for the transport of goods. As for the chariots, at first they were used only for hunting and as mobile command vehicles in battles, but as the Shang Dynasty was approaching its end, the use of chariots in battles became more widespread and more directly used, participating in a fight instead of just staying in the back merely as a command post.

It was also during the rule of the Shang that war and military became more important and better organized even though the size of their armies, usually ranging from three to five thousand and rarely going up to ten thousand, wasn't that impressive. Most of the warriors were foot soldiers armed with axes, spears, and bows. At the core of these armies stood a small number of trained noble professionals, which can be attested by the existence of various titles and ranks, who spent their lives honing their fighting skills. And they most likely protected the king or the general in charge. The majority of the troops came from untrained peasant levies raised from the subordinate noble lineages called zu. These linages served as both military and social organizations, which give us glimpses into how the Shang state and society was organized. It was, in fact, a semi-feudal patriarchal lineage system in which royal lineage ruled over the smaller local families that were to serve their king. Lineage heads of these zu were interconnected with the royal dynasty through various kinship ties, benefits, privileges, and obligations. Kings offered them spiritual guidance, performing religious rituals for them, and protection for their service in his armies and for the tributes they paid. It becomes obvious that the Shang state still didn't have fully developed bureaucracy, as it depended on the local aristocracy to fulfill the will of the central government even though there were some royal offices, usually given to the higher nobles trusted by the king, like "junior servitor for cultivation." The question remains if these proto-bureaucratic offices actually held any power or were only ceremonial.

Another thing that this patriarchal social system also tells us is that the ancient Chinese kings served an important religious role in society. Calling upon their connection with their deified and worshiped ancestors, the Shang rulers managed to play a central role in the religious life of their subjects, which was an important cornerstone of their control over the subjects they ruled. This made early Chinese kings' rule rather theocratic, as it was with many other ancient kings, for example, the pharaohs in Egypt. This role of the king as a royal shaman, of course, decreased as their political power and wealth rose, as they no longer needed to rely as much upon spiritual control of the people beneath them. But despite that, religion continued to play an important role in the everyday life of Shang China. Sacrifices were a common practice for them, and though most of the offerings were animals or valuable items, in some cases there are signs of human sacrifices, mostly in royal tombs, possibly to serve the kings in the afterlife. And even in death, they preserved the hierarchy, with the closest retainers of the ruler being buried closest to him. Farthest away were dismembered and decapitated young men, most likely prisoners of war.

7. Oracle bones carved with earliest found evidence of the Chinese script.
  Source

: https://commons.wikimedia.org

Divination seemed to be one of the most important segments of their belief system and practices, where the shamans would try to speak with the gods and the ancestors, asking for their advice and favors. The importance of this practice is corroborated by the fact that the earliest evidence of the Chinese script comes from 13ᵗʰ century BCE oracle bones, where they would inscribe records and question which would then be burned and interpreted by a soothsayer through pyromantic divinations. Using written words for divination, at the time when literacy was uncommon and script was seen as something special and almost magical, means that this practice had a special significance for the ancient Chinese. And as bones are long-lasting materials, those writings were preserved from being lost in memory.

The fact that there was a fully developed writing system during the Shang rule is also indicative of how far the Chinese civilization had advanced by that point. Now it should be mentioned that it is most likely that the ancient Chinese had developed writing well before the 13ᵗʰ century, as by that time it was already a fully functional and organized system, with some historians arguing that the first versions of the Chinese script had been developed during the Xia Dynasty. But as no archeological evidence for that has been found, at this point it's only conjecture. Also, it should be noted that writing most likely wasn't used only for religious purposes, at least by the golden age of the Shang Dynasty. As their state was at that point rather large, with various tributes being paid and levies being raised, they needed to keep some records of all state business. Some evidence found in the script itself points to the possibility of non-religious documents being written on less durable materials like bamboo, wood, or even cloth, making their survival to the present day rather unlikely. But the fact remains that Chinese culture had advanced significantly by the late 2ⁿᵈ millennium BCE, attested not only by writing but with all the other achievements of the Shang Dynasty.

But as it is often the case in history, after a great ruler and a golden age, states usually start declining and the central government slowly loses its power. As time progressed, new kings of the Shang Dynasty were less and less involved with the ruling, delegating more and more to their officers. They were no longer generals leading their troops, and they no longer worried about the general wellbeing of their subjects, leaving their representatives to deal with droughts or famine. And as their grip loosened, with their focus on indulgence instead of ruling, vassals and subjects started to slowly slip away from their control. First farther away from the Shang core territory, then closer to home. One of these rogue vassals was the noble Zhou family, which ruled in the western borders of the Shang state. They became so powerful, almost to the point of being an independent state, that eventually the head of the family named Wen was imprisoned by a Shang king called Di Xin. He feared Wen's influence and might. As retribution, Wen planned to overthrow the Shang king, who in his youth was a rather good and capable ruler, but who became more and more careless and cruel in his older age. Yet Wen died before following through with his plans. But his son Wu fulfilled his father wishes.

As a king, Di Xin was unaware of just how bad the state of his dominion was, so he sent an army to battle in the east. Wu exploited this and attacked the core of the Shang territory, and according to traditional sources, he was backed by many former allies and loyal vassals of the decaying Shang Dynasty. In 1046 BCE, the grand battle of Muye ensued in which forces of Di Xin suffered a complete defeat. He fled to one of his palaces where he set himself on fire, committing suicide. With his death, Wu became the new king, creating a new dynasty called Zhou. And the old Shang king, who became one of the examples of a bad and corrupt ruler, actually became known as King Zhou, which when written in different Chinese characters and pronounced differently means horse crupper, a part of the saddle which was most often soiled by the horse. At this point, it seemed that the rule of the new Zhou Dynasty was secured, as most of the people welcomed the change on the throne, especially as the new king immediately opened royal warehouses to help the troubled commoners and gain their support. But only two years after his great victory, King Wu died, leaving only his rather young son named Song to rule.

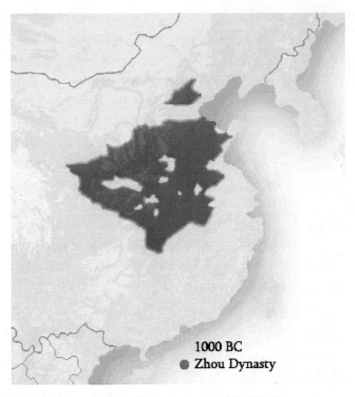

1000 BC
● Zhou Dynasty

*8. Territory under Zhou rule around 1000 BCE Source:
https://commons.wikimedia.org*

Fearing that a young king may be a liability on the throne as the Zhou Dynasty rule was not yet cemented, his uncle Gong Dan stepped in as his guardian and regent, ruling in his place. But it seems this was Gong Dan's sole decision as other brothers of the late king Wu were angered by his move, as at least one of them had seniority in the succession line. This led to a civil war between brothers. On one side was Gong Dan and King Cheng, as Song became later known, and the "Three Guards," Gong Dan's brothers. And although the Guards were also backed by other nobles and the remnants of the Shang Dynasty, in the end, they were unable to beat Gong Dan. He used his power not only to confirm the rule of the Zhou Dynasty but also to expand its territory. And when young King Cheng became old enough, he willingly stepped down, leaving the throne to his nephew, but still remained an important part of the royal council. As such, he was remembered in the next generations as the paragon of virtue, sometimes even called The First Sage. But more importantly, some modern historians credit him for formulating the political doctrine known as the Mandate of Heaven.

That doctrine was used to legitimize the overthrowing of the Shang Dynasty and the formation of the new Zhou Dynasty. It stipulated that every dynasty and its current ruler had been given a mandate by heaven to rule in the natural order, for the benefit of the entire nation. If any ruler failed to do so, he could be rightfully dethroned and substituted by another, even substituting an entire dynasty with him. And as the last ruler of the Shang situation was rather terrible, the Zhou had all the right to rebel, as now the mandate from heaven was on their side, which was confirmed by their victory. This doctrine had since those days become one of the most important pillars of the imperial rule, which was upheld by all following dynasties going up to the 20th century and the modern age. It has been used by Chinese kings and emperors to both stabilize and consolidate their rule, as well as a justification to overthrow their predecessors. It is worth mentioning that though this was the first official proclamation of this doctrine, its roots can be traced to the stories of how the Shang overthrew the Xia Dynasty for their maleficent rule.

But the Zhou Dynasty did more than just rely on a new political doctrine to secure its newly acquired power. First, kings recognized that one of the weaknesses of the Shang state was disloyalty of the vassals, which had little real ties to the central government. The Zhou rulers realized that relying on religion and offering protection wasn't going to buy them much loyalty, so they confiscated and divided a lot of lands among their next of kin, to the brothers and sons of kings Wu and Cheng, as well as Gong Dan. This created dozens of smaller city-states, which were closely connected to the central dynasty by blood. This kind of decentralized rule, where local lords govern their own estates with only partial subordination to the central government, is sometimes equated to the medieval

European feudalism, but that is not the case here. This system, known as fēngjiàn, was more based on familial ties than on the feudal code. And at best it could be described as proto-feudalism. And indeed, it brought a few decades of peace and prosperity in China, without many rivalries and fights among the nobles, as they did not challenge the authority of the central government.

9. King Zhao of Zhou. Source: https://commons.wikimedia.org

This early period is marked by the expansion and conquest of the neighboring tribes to the north and the east. And these newly conquered lands weren't just forced into vassalage, as was the custom before. The new dynasty tried to maintain a higher level of control and loyalty from these areas by colonizing them, giving the local rule to their family members and relocating some of the loyal population with them. It was a sign that the new fēngjiàn system was functioning, as the Zhou state became more powerful, wealthier, and larger than their Shang predecessor. But in the mid-10th century BCE, under the rule of King Zhao, who ruled from 977 to 957, expansion was halted. He tried to continue in the footsteps of his father and grandfather, but he suffered a decisive defeat in his campaign in the south. The Zhou Dynasty lost both its ruler and the majority of the core royal forces. Zhao's successor king, Mu, found himself in a tough position. The central government lost both its might and its reputation among their subjects. At the same time, due to the changing of generations, the blood connection between the king and his vassals thinned down, as the ties were no longer as close as brothers and uncles; now they became distant cousins twice or thrice removed. The Zhou proto-feudal system was starting to crack.

And it seems that King Mu was aware of that as he worked hard to reform the state, starting with the army. He realized that it would be more beneficial if he chose his captains and generals according to their abilities rather than due to their familial ties. Thus, he started the practice of investiture in the army, which marked a start of Chinese military restructuring and a gradual turn toward professionalization. Mu used a similar idea when he reformed his court as well. He gathered capable people around him to act as his ministers or, as they were titled, supervisors, alongside numerous scribes, attendants, and provisioners. Thus, a bureaucratic apparatus was created that started to separate the king from his people, even the nobles. This could be clearly seen in the fact that during his reign all visitors of the royal court had to be introduced to the king who no longer knew all of his vassals personally. Furthermore, King Mu started the practice of writing down every court decision, ruling, maps, investitures, laws, and any other royal action. By doing that, he created the first systematical legal code in China.

These reforms allowed King Mu to spend most of his long rule in campaigns with his army. He waged wars on pretty much all fronts. He defended then expanded the western and northern borders, confirmed the royal influence in the east, and led a successful invasion in the southeast. He was rather successful in those military actions, as under his rule the Zhou state achieved its greatest extent. He managed to conquer numerous tribes either by swaying their allegiance with the showing of the royal force or through pure conquest if they refused to comply. But despite his military success and important reforms, he wasn't seen as a great ruler. On the one hand, he received due praise for his achievements but on the other, he was criticized for being away from the capital too often, and that his legal and bureaucratic reforms were needed because he lacked the virtues and charisma of previous rulers. And during his reign, the rule of the kings became a faceless, distant administrative system which cared less for the people. Even his military achievements were seen only as a partial success as one of the larger border states stopped being a royal vassal.

Yet despite the flaws of King Mu, he did manage to keep his rule mostly stable, and the central government retained both influence and power. But during the next half-century and the next four Chinese kings, those things slowly but surely changed. Though exact chronology and events can't be precisely dated, certain stories give us glimpses into how the general state of affairs developed. One of the most important eastern vassals was boiled in oil, and on several occasions, the royal army had to interfere in local affairs of the nobles. This means that the control of the central government was deteriorating and that now it had to rely on brute force to enforce its own will. Some of the vassals even dared attack the royal lands. At the same time, surrounding tribes were also using the weakened state of China as a reason to attack it. Later sources tell us that the royal house started to decline, even being ridiculed by satires of poets. The culmination of that deterioration came during the rule of King Li in the mid-9th century BCE.

King Li was a terrible king, corrupt and decadent, without a single redeeming quality. He cared little about his subjects, refused to listen to the advice of his court officials or other nobles, seeking only ways to gather more wealth. King Li was also cruel, severely punishing anyone who dared to speak out against him. Things became so unbearable that finally some of the nobles started an open revolt against the Zhou, forcing King Li into exile in 841 BCE. The period that ensued is today known as the Gonghe (joint harmony) Regency where the Chinese throne was factually empty. During this interregnum, it seems that a certain Gong He ruled as a regent, though some sources also mentioned a combined rule of Shao Gong and Zhou Gong. But even if the latter two weren't ruling, they played an important role at the time as in 828, when King Li died in exile, they persuaded Gong He to give up the rule in favor of Li's son, the future king Xuan. The Gonghe Regency gives us a sure clue how weakened the royal power had become by that time and how powerful the nobles became. But despite that, some of the royal prestige and significance remained, otherwise Xuan wouldn't have been chosen to rule, as Gong He was in a good position to start a new dynasty. Most likely he wasn't able to do so as other nobles would have opposed him.

Whatever may be the actual reason, King Xuan assumed the throne, and at first, he seemed like the capable and strong leader the Zhou needed to recover from the interregnum. In the first third of his 45-year rule, he achieved substantial victories in the west and the south, while he managed to reaffirm the Zhou control in the east. His main goal was to restore the royal authority, and it seemed he was going to achieve it. But as the years passed, the Zhou king once again got the military involved in succession matters of the local lords on several occasions. It is likely that he was trying to ensure that his supporters and people more loyal to him would inherit the titles, thus widening the support he had among the nobles. But this plan backfired, and after these interventions, most of the nobles started rebelling, refusing to carry out orders that came from the king and the central government. This eventually led to his downfall, as he stepped out of line by killing an innocent nobleman. Legends say King Xuan was eventually killed by the angry ghost of the murdered noble, but in reality, it was most likely assassination in retribution for the vile act. So, in 782 BCE he was succeeded by his son, You.

10. *King Xuan of Zhou. Source: https://commons.wikimedia.org*

The reign of the new king started rather ominously as a major earthquake caused massive damage in the second year of his rule. Sources tell us that mountains crumbled and rivers dried out, and even though this is most likely an exaggeration, it shows that there were severe consequences of this natural disaster. To make matters worse, he caused troubles in his court as he chased off his queen and heir, who came from an important noble family, in favor of a concubine and a son he had with her. Traditional histories tell us that furthermore King You toyed with the remaining loyal nobles by lighting alarm beacons for the amusement of his concubine queen. And soon no one answered the call of the alarm. So, when in 771 BCE the former queen's family colluded with the western barbarian tribes, which were a constant threat for the Zhou capital for decades, and attacked, no one came to help the foolish king. He was murdered, and the capital was ransacked and devastated. With the death of King You, the main branch of the Zhou Dynasty was now extinguished, and Ping, the son of the banished queen, became the new king. Since the region was brutally sacked by the barbarians, the capital was moved to the east, where one of the early Zhou colonies were created. This marks a fall of the so-called Western Zhou and the start of the Eastern Zhou Dynasty.

Even though in reality the same dynasty remained in power, many modern historians see this moment as pivotal in the further development of Chinese history. With a new king, a new capital, and rather important changes in royal power, historians tend to divide the Zhou rule into two separate periods. As it will become clear in the next chapter, during the Eastern Zhou rule, royal power and dynastic prestige would continue to fade, leaving only an empty shell of its former glory. But despite that ungraceful development, the early Western Zhou rulers did leave an important mark on China and its political development. Under their almost three centuries-long rule, the dogma of the government property and control, political thoughts and doctrines, and even of poetic expressions were established. All of this became embedded into the Chinese culture and intellectual thought, present even today in some form. And if the Xia and Shang Dynasties were the foundations of the Chinese civilization, often unseen and buried under the soil of forgotten history, the Western Zhou are a visible and recognizable cornerstone, marking the base of future Chinese grandeur. And for that they deserved, and indeed received, eternal praise of the Chinese people.

Chapter 3 – Disintegration of Royal Power

Despite the fact that the Eastern Zhou survived, carrying on the traditions set by the early Zhou kings, by the late 8th century BCE, it became clear that the royal power of the ruling dynasty had all but disappeared. In fact, for the most part of the next five centuries, Zhou rulers were mostly only puppets on the throne, while the real power lay with local nobles ruling the several large states. This is why historians sometimes disregard the Eastern Zhou Dynasty, dividing their formal rule into two periods. First was the Autumn and Spring Period, named after the Spring and Autumn Annals, which describe the period between 722 and 481 in which nobles competed for the influence over the king. The other period is known as the Warring States Period, which lasted until 221, in which the nobles openly fought amongst themselves for full control of China, without much regard for the actual Zhou ruler. But the disintegration of the royal power started in 771 when the capital was moved to the east and when the core Zhou lands were abandoned by the king.

King Ping, who was responsible for the relocation of the royal capital, in the early days of his reign, forged an alliance with one of the more important noble families called Zheng. In fact, the Zheng forces protected the court while it was moving to the east, and later they defended royal lands from the barbarian invasion. But at the same time, the Zheng duke disregarded any formal relations between him and his liege, attacking other Zhou vassals. Ping tried to balance Zheng power by appointing another mighty noble, the Duke of Guo, to an important court minister office. The Duke of Zheng was enraged, and in an attempt to pacify him, the Zhou king proposed an exchange of hostages between him and the duke. This was an unheard-of precedent in the fēngjiàn feudal system, showing once more how the royal power had wavered.

In 719, Ping died, and his son Huan became the new king. Like his father, he feared the might of the Zheng duke, so he tried once again to limit his influence by placing a Guo noble as his chief minister. This time the Duke of Zheng responded by openly attacking the king's lands. In response, King Huan gathered forces of several other vassals and in 707 fought against the rebellious duke. The Zhou forces were defeated, and this marked the end of any kind of royal authority, especially as the king himself was wounded. That fact meant that the Zhou kings lost their status as the Sons of Heaven.

It was in this political atmosphere that the rule of Eastern Zhou started, with about 150 independent states only formally subordinated to the kings. Of course, most of these states were rather small, consisting of only one city and its immediate surroundings. Most of these smaller states were annexed by one of the fifteen larger states. And out of those fifteen, only the Chu, Jin, Qi, and Qin states were constantly competing for the leading role among the states, for power, influence, and prestige during the Autumn and Spring Period. Of course, the other states were also involved as allies and foes, or simply as battlegrounds between the major powers. And as before, they were all surrounded by the barbarian tribes which were a constant threat to the Chinese states, but also possible allies in the struggle for power. The Duke of Zheng tried to enforce himself as the de facto leader of China after his victory over the Zhou forces, but he died before he could fully achieve that. And as he had many sons, his successors started fighting amongst themselves as who would become the next Duke of Zheng. Rather quickly, other states got involved in these skirmishes as well. That civil war, combined with lack of any signs of Zhou power, prompted several barbarian tribes to invade the Yellow River Valley.

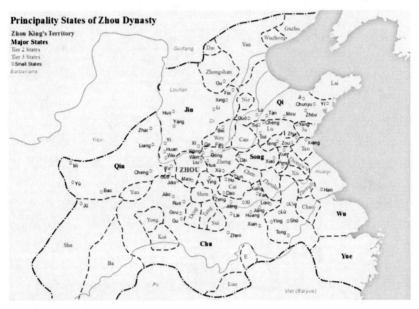

11. Map of states and territories of the Eastern Zhou period. Source: https://commons.wikimedia.org

But where the Duke of Zheng failed, the Duke Huan of Qi succeeded. In 685 BCE, he became the duke of the eastern state of Qi, and with the help of his chief minister, he reformed his domain. With a more hierarchical administration, which was now better organized and more efficient, Qi became capable of mobilizing human and material resources better than any other state, making it the most powerful in the entire Chinese realm. By 667, Duke Huan was powerful enough to gather rulers of four other states which all pledged allegiance to him. At the same time, the Zhou King Hui had been challenged by his brother for the throne. Seeing how Duke

Huan was the most powerful leader, he asked for his assistance in exchange for a title he created just for him, the title of ba (hegemon). Huan accepted, as that title legally recognized his leadership among the Chinese states, and it gave him the right to intervene militarily in the name of the royal court as he pleased. Though this would seem like a usurpation of the royal power, it seems Duke Huan and his chief minister didn't plan for that. The goal of their hegemony was to preserve the Zhou feudal system and restore the authority of the Son of Heaven.

The actions of Duke of Qi, in essence, corroborate these intentions as he attacked a state that supported the king's brother, sent armies to help smaller states against the barbarian invaders, and even helped reestablish several states that had been practically destroyed by the foreign invaders. These actions cemented his place as the head of the Chinese states. But at the same time, the southern state of Chu, which remained outside of the Zhou feudal system, grew stronger and started to expand to the north. It became a serious threat to all the other states, so in 656, Duke Huan led an allied army of eight northern states against them, beating them in open battle. With that victory, he forced Chu to negotiate, stopping their expansion for the time being. But the biggest success of the Duke of Qi was a series of interstate meetings, the most important being the one held in 651 in Kuiqui. There several major states agreed to respect the patriarchal traditions of old, attempting to stop the political chaos when it came to the question of succession. They also agreed upon respecting each other's boundaries, preserving irrigation systems, and promoting the trade of grain, which was aimed at improving state relations. But at the same time, an agreement made at Kuiqui stipulated that no administrative office should be hereditary, promoting the meritocratic system against the old feudal ideals.

Unfortunately for Qi, Duke Huan died in 643, leaving behind six sons who immediately started fighting for succession despite their father's attempts to prevent exactly that. For that, the state of Qi lost its place as the hegemon. It was unofficially succeeded by the state of Song, led by Duke Xiang. For a short period, the state of Song was the most powerful, even intervening in matters of succession in Qi. But in 638, Xiang attempted, against the advice of his officers, to lead his army against the state of Chu. He was defeated, dying a year later from the wounds sustained in battle, and Song's power was destroyed. But despite the fact Xiang never officially received the title of ba from the Zhou king, his attempts to continue in the footsteps of Duke Huan led the ensuing generations of Chinese to count him as one of the Zhou hegemons. During the same period, the northern state of Jin also went through reforms under the rule of Duke Wen, and it rapidly became one of the most powerful Chinese states. So, in 635 when King Xiang needed an ally to keep his throne in a struggle with his brother, Wen was glad to help. Then he led the allied army against the invading forces of Chu in 633 and achieved an important victory. That helped earn him the title of hegemon in 632.

In his attempts to retain a balance of power, the leader of Jin fought off the expansion of the Qin state to the east. But Duke Wen died shortly after in 628, and Duke Mu of Qin exploited that and continued his expansion, achieving a major victory over the state of Jin in 624. Like the previous hegemon states, Qin also went through reforms before achieving its supremacy, no matter how short it lasted. Its core lands were in the valley of the Wei River, where the Western Zhou Dynasty was situated before. As such, it managed to expand both to the barbarian tribes to the west as well as to the smaller states that lay to the east of it. Once again, Duke Mu was never officially recognized as a hegemon, but his superiority until his death in 621 made later generations recognize him as one. From that point onward, it seems that no state managed to gain the upper hand as all skirmishes between Qi, Qin, and Jin ended without a decisive victory. And soon after the southern state of Chu was once again advancing to the north, under the rule of self-proclaimed king Zhuang. In 598, he managed to defeat the forces of Jin and even endangered the realm of the Zhou king. But despite the fact that the leader of Chu was the most powerful of all the rulers, he also didn't receive official recognition but is still counted as one of the hegemons, like several rulers before him.

He died in 591, and the struggle for power continued with all of the four most powerful states being approximately equal in power and influence, especially when the state of Jin connected with the state of Wu in the lower reaches of the Yangzi River. This state before this point was seen as barbaric and wasn't part of Chinese civilizational reach. But Jin saw potential in it, helping it with arms and technology so it could threaten the state of Chu on a new front. But this wasn't enough to stop the ever-growing power of Chu, so in 580 BCE, the state of Jin managed to once again forge an alliance with Qi and Qin to fight against the southern threat. With that, the four major states were in a deadlock, and the state of Song that was caught between them convinced them to arrange a meeting the following year. There they agreed on peace and disarmament, limiting their military powers, which is one of the earliest records of this kind of agreement. Yet it was short-lived as by 575 the full-scale war continued with a victory for Jin and its allies against Chu. Under the rule of a new duke named Dao, the state of Jin went through a new set of reforms, further developing a meritocratic administrative system. That gave this state internal stability, and its achievements against the Chu and some barbarian tribes was enough for Dao to become the next ba.

But by that time, the Zhou kings lost any kind of respect to other dukes and rulers, so his title of hegemon meant almost nothing anymore. And the fighting continued over the next several decades. This kind of never-ending warfare became rather exhausting, especially for the smaller states that served as little more than the battlefields for the major powers, and this led to another meeting of the four major powers in 546. However, this time they were accompanied by several smaller states as well. There, in essence, the spheres of influence of these states were agreed upon, and peace among them ensued for several decades with only smaller skirmishes among their vassals. But by no means did this mean ultimate peace was achieved. Despite peace on its northern borders, Chu had to fight in the south against former allies of Jin, the state of Wu. For a long time, Wu harassed the bordering provinces of Chu, slowly exhausting its enemy. By 506, the state of Wu felt powerful enough to launch a full-scale attack on Chu, bringing it on the verge of collapse in the next couple of years. But before the final blow was struck, the Wu capital was attacked by Yue forces, another new power in the southern edges of the Chinese world.

This forced the ruler of Wu, who like the rulers of Chu held the title of king which wasn't recognized by the dukes of the northern states, to rush back and defend his land. He succeeded but died from the wounds sustained from the fight. His son, King Fuchai, avenged his father in 494. He forced the king of Yue to surrender to him. With secure southern borders, the army of Wu marched to the north. There they fought against the forces of Qi and won, while at the same time Fuchai attempted to build a canal to connect the Central Plain, which is another name for the region between the Yellow and Yangtze Rivers, with the southern states. This was a direct challenge to Jin, the most powerful northern state, which yielded, deciding not to confront the mighty army of Wu. This prompted King Fuchai to preside over an interstate conference in 482 where he was awarded the title of ba. But while his armies were busy in the north, the king of Yue launched a new attack on the capital of Wu, prompting the king of Wu to rush back south once more. His new title meant nothing when his forces were defeated by King Goujian of Yue. The Yue forces did retreat after a peace treaty, but King Goujian didn't want to let Wu recuperate from the defeat, so soon after he launched a new invasion. By 473, Wu was completely defeated, and Fuchai committed suicide. Afterward, Goujian marched north and was recognized as the new hegemon. But this title lost almost all of its weight, and with his death in 465 BCE, the ba system came to an end.

12. Spear of King Fuchai of Wu. Source: https://commons.wikimedia.org

With the disintegration of the ba system, the disappearance of over 120 smaller states, and the total annihilation of royal authority, the Spring and Autumn Period ended. The exact end year is debated among historians, ranging from 481 to 403 BCE, but most commonly the year used is the one proposed by the ancient Chinese historian, Sima Qian, who said it happened in 476. But the year isn't what is really important, but how Chinese civilization changed in those three centuries. Maybe most importantly, the old familial feudal system was largely abolished and substituted by a meritocratic system, even for higher court official positions and the most important fiefs, as the most capable people became ministers that in some cases played an important role in the development of the states they served. And later on, as there was less and less land to give, it became harder for new aristocratic families to rise, making it a rather closed circle.

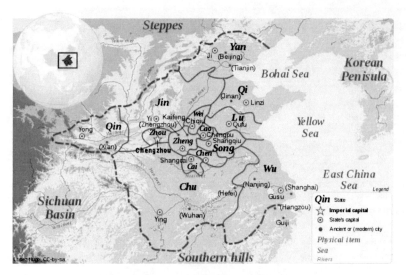

*13. States of the late Spring and Autumn Period. Source:
https://commons.wikimedia.org*

Another step away from the feudal system was the development of
an advanced administrative system, where the meritocratic system
was most useful. State territories were divided into a number of
smaller administrative regions ruled by governors who directly
answered to the ruler, and whose office wasn't hereditary. They were
helped by local administrative personnel, like sheriffs and stewards.
This was important because it made levying the troops easier as well
as broader, giving dukes and kings of the late Spring and Autumn
Period much larger armies at their disposal. This stems from the fact
that in earlier times they could levy troops only from their capital,
but now the entire land was at their disposal. But probably more
important than that was the fact that this kind of advanced
administrative system allowed for better taxation, allowing for more
money to flow into the rulers' treasuries. This was accompanied by
reforming the taxes so that the sum the state required depended on
the size of arable land. Amount of levied taxes also rose with the
increase of farming output that happened during this period. One of
the reasons for this was, once again, because the old feudal system
was failing. In the old Zhou system, in theory, all land belonged to
the king, and peasants had little incentive to work harder than they

had to. But as the royal authority disappeared, slowly farmers gained the right of tenure and later even ownership, making them more productive. This was coupled with the advances in farming techniques and technologies that also happened in this period. Among those was harnessing animals, mainly oxen, to pull the plows, allowing for deeper cuts into the soil. Coupled with that was the use of metal iron tools, which also made farming more efficient.

That fact also tells us that during this period China was transitioning from the Bronze Age to the Iron Age, though this transformation was not yet complete. At the time, iron was still of a lesser quality, and it was mostly used for tools, while bronze was considered "fine metal." As such, it was still used for weapons and ceremonial items. But both types of metal were made with the casting technology, which made mass production easier. They were melted and produced in kilns that could reach up to 1300°C (2370°F). Not coincidentally, during this same period, pottery techniques advanced enough for its products to be called ceramics. And in most cities from this period, archeologist have found remains of bronze-making and pottery workshops, meaning that these industries, if it's possible to call them that, were an important part of economic life in ancient China. With more food surpluses and new "industrial" products came the rise of commerce, which also became an important part of the late Spring and Autumn Period. Development of trade also pushed for further improvements of the road networks which were secured and maintained by the state. The active exchange of material wealth through commerce also gave rise to an important advance in the Chinese civilization, the appearance of money, or to be more precise, minted coins. This helped to further improve trade and circulation of wealth, making economic life in ancient China livelier, pushing states into new heights.

14. Bronze polearm head of the Spring and Autumn Period. Source: https://commons.wikimedia.org

All of these changes were accompanied by the change of Chinese philosophical and political thought. With state administration growing ever more complex and needing qualified people to run it, members of the elite slowly started to shift from a purely warrior class to a more intellectual one. And from that pool of talent, the best were chosen, thanks to the meritocratic system, to serve as high-ranking officers. Thanks to this, they were able to spearhead the intellectual development of ancient China. The best example of this is, of course, the world-famous Confucius, who served the state of Lu and managed to create a universal code of conduct applicable to everyone based on his interpretation of traditions and old feudal customs. His thoughts became one of the pillars of Chinese civilization, which still remains today. But despite the traditionalism he proclaimed, his thoughts were innovative and represented a more pragmatic approach in the Chinese political and intellectual thought. This can be corroborated by the fact that the old traditions, like relying on shamans to overcome droughts or on legends and customs to keep society in line, were weakening and losing their place in Chinese civilization. Instead, Confucianism rather relied on written codes of law. In general, it could be said that pragmatism started to permeate the Chinese society in the Spring and Autumn Period. But this civilization was only halfway through the processes of all of these changes, which were going to culminate in the next era, today known as the Warring States Period.

Chapter 4 – Birth of Imperial China

Though the Spring and Autumn Period seemed like a never-ending conflict between the Chinese states, it was actually a gradual preparation for a major escalation of warfare which culminated in the next epoch in Chinese history. It became known as the Warring States Period because the essence of war changed during it with battles becoming bloodier and campaigns lasting longer. Under that kind of pressure, the nature of the states changed as well, as they became territorial and bureaucratic in nature. Their number was further reduced as smaller states continued to be sucked in by the more powerful states. And while in the previous period there were only four major powers among the Chinese states, during the Warring States era their number rose to seven. These were Qin, Qi, Chu, Yan, Han, Zhao, and Wei. This period was characterized by large-scale warfare and alliances among these major states, three of which were old powers from the previous period.

At the beginning of this period, probably the most influential of the major states was the state of Qi, on the shores of present-day Bohai Sea, covering the area of modern Chinese provinces of Shandong and Hebei. Then there was the state of Chu in the south, covering an area around the Huai and Yangtze Rivers. In the west was Qin, located in the basin of the Wei River, which later expanded to the parts of the modern-day Sichuan province. Then there was a new major power in the north, around present-day Beijing, called the state of Yan, and it was the last state to emerge as a powerhouse. The final three were formed during the second half of the 5th century in a long process today known as the partition of Jin. This state, which throughout the Spring and Autumn Period was usually the most powerful, got mixed up in a long civil war that lasted from about 458 to 403, when three leading aristocratic families were recognized by the Zhou king, as well as other states, as equals. The smallest of these emerging states was Han, which covered the southern parts of modern-day Shanxi and Henan provinces. The second successor of Jin was the state of Zhao, located on the northern borders of China, on the borders of present-day Inner Mongolia and the northern parts of Shanxi provinces. And finally, the most powerful heir of Jin was Wei, a state located north of the Yellow River and in the valley of the Fen River, covering an area of the modern-day central Shanxi province, as well as parts of the Henan and Hebei provinces.

The early decades of the Warring States Period were marked by further reforms that started in the previous century that finally transformed Chinese states one by one into ruler-centered states. This meant that dukes became the sole source of authority in their states. The last states to achieve this kind of centralization of power were Qin, who gained it only at the beginning of the 4th century, and Yan, where these reforms were conducted at the end of that century. An exception was the state of Chu which never became fully ruler-centered, as they had a mixed strength with royal authority. This weakness was compensated by the sheer size of this southern state, which throughout this period remained the largest. Of course, this period was also marked by wars and skirmishes between the major states and their expansions, both through conquering remaining smaller states and through expanding into the "barbarian wilderness." The first state to benefit from the reforms was Qi, who in the mid-4th century managed to affirm itself as the strongest state after significant victories over Wei and Yen. But the most important result of these victories was the fact that in 344 rulers of Qi and Wei mutually recognized each other as kings, finally showing that the Zhou Dynasty lost the last remnants of its importance. From this point on, all states were interlocked in a fight to become the new supreme ruler of all Chinese states.

The Situation of Early Warring States Period

15. *Map of China in the early Warring States Period. Source:*
https://commons.wikimedia.org

But the higher ranked ruler state of Wei was actually going through a period of crisis, as the reformed and more powerful Qin started attacking it from the west. It suffered several defeats in the mid-4th century and had to rely on Qi to stop Qin from completely conquering it in 340. With this, the two most powerful states in ancient China became Qin and Qi. As a result, in 325, the ruler of Qin proclaimed himself king as well, and soon he was followed by rulers of Han, Zhao, and Yan in the next two years. And as rulers of Chu bore the unrecognized title of kings since the 7th century, this meant that all of the major states were now officially kingdoms, and they recognized each other in that way. What little dignity left for the Zhou kings was destroyed in the following years when rulers of smaller states, like Song and Zhongshan, also proclaimed themselves kings. Interestingly, after a considerable defeat of Zhao in a war with Qin in 318, the king of that state retracted his proclamation, returning his title to a level of a duke. Despite that, his son and successor held a tile of a king. Meanwhile, in the south, the state of Chu was conquering its only contender in the Yangtze River Valley, the state of You, strengthening its position.

By the late 4th and early 3rd century, the state of Qin grew to become the number one power in China that no other state, not even Chu or Qi, could match in a direct fight. This rise in might didn't just come from the state and military reforms, but mostly as a result of expansion in present-day Sichuan. This land in the upper region of the Yangtze River was rather fertile, giving a boost to the Qin economy and providing a fresh source of new troops. As a bonus, their lands were rather secure by mountain ranges, especially the new territories, so their lands suffered almost no damage from foreign invasions. And finally, the geographical location of Qin meant that it could fight a war only on two fronts, going east toward the Yellow River and the Central Plain or going down the Yangtze River, threatening the core lands of Chu. This prompted other states to revise their tactics and diplomacies. They realized that the Qin threat was too great for them to singlehandedly defeat themselves; thus, the century of alliances began. Two main diplomatic doctrines were the so-called vertical and horizontal alliances. The vertical alliances involved the states on the north-south axis to unitedly act against the Qin. Opposed to it was the horizontal alliance, where states allied with Qin to reap the fruits of Qin supremacy for themselves, as well as to protect their lands from Qin attacks.

But by no means does this mean that Qin was unbeatable. Though the first allied attack in 318 was a failure, the succession crisis in 307 weakened the position of Qin. This was exploited by King Min of Qi, who led an alliance attack on Qin in 298. After a few years of struggle, Qin had to yield, asking for peace, and in return, it gave portions of its western territories to Wei and Han. Continuing on that success, Qi attacked Yen and Chu as well, marking a short period of restoration of Qi power. Following some internal struggles, Qi abandoned its alliance with Wei and Han while at the same time it achieved a temporary truce with Qin. Several years later, in 288, the kings of these two states met up, and for the first time in Chinese history declared themselves di (emperors) of the west and the east, a title which was in the past preserved only for mythological semi-god rulers. This was a clear political statement for everyone about what the ultimate goal was for every king fighting in the late Warring States Period. Together, the two self-proclaimed emperors plotted to attack Zhao, but Min of Qi was persuaded by others that this would only benefit Qin at the cost of Qi supremacy. So, he backed out of the alliance and formed a new one, now aimed against Qin.

This forced the Qin ruler, Zhao, to abdicate his new title, which Min had already abandoned, and give up the territories he took from Wei and Zhao. The following year, Qi attacked and annexed Song, one of the last remaining smaller states. This kind of rise had become too alarming for other states to ignore, and in 284, Qi was simultaneously attacked by Yen, Qin, Zhao, Wei, and Han. Chou declared itself an ally of Qi, but only to retake the lands it lost around the Huai River. Qi suffered a total defeat, with the death of King Min and the destruction of all of its armies. Qi territories were occupied until 279 when they managed to regain them, but Qi was never again able to achieve its former power. But this shifting of powers and alliances was best used by the state of Zhao, which was altering its allegiance between Qi and Qin. As such, it managed to expand its territories at the expense of Wei and Qi. This expansion, coupled with military reforms, propelled Zhao to be the most powerful state in the ensuing decade, achieving several victories over Qin by 269. These defeats caused the king Zhao of Qin to change his state policies and philosophy of war.

16. Statue of a Qin soldier. Source: https://commons.wikimedia.org

His advisors pointed out to him that fighting solely for supremacy and waging war against the strongest opponent was futile, as they had seen in their experience with Qi and Zhao. So, the king of Qin decided to abandon the old system of alliances in favor of diplomacy based on a maxim "alliance with the distant and war with the neighbor." This way of thinking was aimed at achieving irreversible expansion of a state, with all new territory gains belonging solely to the king, not his generals or vassals. The sole aim of war for Qin became territorial gain. Furthermore, he stated his policy of attacking not only the lands of the enemy but people as well. This meant that the ultimate goal, besides expansion of the state, was annihilating rival armies so that enemy states would lose any capacity of fighting. But this kind of military thought wasn't developed just overnight. Over two centuries leading up to this point, armies were slowly growing from at most 30,000 at the beginning of this era to 300,000 in the last decades. Scholars today presume that these records were overexaggerated, but they clearly show an increase in the scale of warfare. With that came casualties that numbered in tens of thousands of dead and wounded.

But these high numbers of fallen soldiers aren't solely explainable by just the sheer size of the armies. Campaigns now lasted for years, not only for a single season. Soldiers were now armed with iron weapons and armor, as it became cheaper and more durable than bronze. New innovations were adapted, like the use of cavalry and crossbows, and in general, there was a substantial advance in military theory, seen in several important writings about it. At the same time, forts and defensive walls around cities became the norm, and with those, various siege techniques were developed, from traction trebuchets to digging tunnels beneath the walls. Battles and sieges became long, and all remains of feudal chivalry were lost by the mid-3rd century. This is best seen in the example of Bai Qi, a Qin general of this era who became known as Ren Tu (human butcher), who in his thirty-year career was responsible for deaths of at least 900,000 enemy soldiers. Some sources even go as high as two million, though this is likely an exaggeration. And the first to bear the Qin attack in 265 was Han, at that point the weakest surviving state and Qin's immediate neighbor. They turned to Zhao for help, which this state eagerly gave. The war dragged on in a stalemate before Qin achieved a grand victory in 260. It seemed that Qin was on the verge of final victory, but exhaustion combined with the loss of several important generals halted its expansion.

17. Qin general Bai Qi. Source: https://commons.wikimedia.org

The next step for King Zhao of Qin was a direct attack on the Zhou Dynasty in 256 BCE. No other state was able or willing to help, and with this, the Zhou lands were conquered and annexed by Qin. That is how the Zhou Dynasty finally ended. Soon afterward, King Zhao died, and after two short rules of older kings, in 247, Zhao Zheng became the new king of Qin. At the time, he was only 13 years old, so he had regents rule in his place until 235. In the first years of his rule, he was preoccupied with securing his place on the throne as he faced a rebellion, but then he started preparing his armies for one last grand campaign. The Qin military machine was finally unleashed in 230. Once again, Han was the first target. Then in 228, Zhao Zheng turned his armies against the Zhao, and in 226 he took parts of Yan. In 225, Wei fell, after which attacks were directed toward Chu, the largest remaining state. But in 223, it also fell without much resistance. The next year, Qin conquered the remaining territories of Yan in the north. And in 221, the last state to be conquered was Qi. After over two centuries of great wars, massive battles, and countless skirmishes, it took less than a decade for Zhao Zheng to achieve complete victory. He crowned his victory by assuming the emperor title huángdì, which he created himself. Thus, he became known as Qin Shi Huangdi, or the First Emperor of Qin. This marks the end of unification and the birth of imperial China.

18. *Illustration of Qin Shi Huangdi from 19th century. Source: https://commons.wikimedia.org*

Ancient China had to go through rather bloody and painful labors to give birth to its first empire, but it would be unjust to speak of this period as one solely marked by wars. With constant pressures from outside and from within, Chinese states and civilization as a whole went through rather impressive advances in almost all fields. First of all, technological advances, fueled by the needs of war, were marked by an already mentioned switch to the use of iron instead of bronze. And continuing the older bronze-working traditions, the iron was also cast. This made it possible for Chinese metalsmiths to mass produce their products. This was rather important for both weapons and for various tools, as they became widespread and cheap enough for the majority to use. That led to the use of iron tools in farming, which in turn led to an increase in food production. This was also accompanied by large-scale irrigation projects, made available by increased logistics and capabilities of central governments, which also proved important for the development of agriculture. So, the Warring States Period, rather paradoxically to all of the carnage caused by such large-scale warfare, was a time of great expansion of the population. This fact is also important to explain why wars did become so massive, as there simply were more people to levy.

Yet advances didn't stop there, as the production of silk was improved which marked the beginning of what we could call the textile industry. Also, transportation was improved as carts with yokes gave way to wagons with shafts and breast harnesses, allowing horses and other tow animals to pull greater weights. At the same time, shipbuilding was also improved. And with improved production in various fields, advances in transportation, and the already mentioned implementation of money, trade also blossomed in the Warring States Period. Merchants became wealthier and held more important ranks of society, with some even managing to gain high-ranking offices in the court. Great cities and capitals were no longer just centers of political power, but also manufacturing and trading hubs.

However, not all advancements in this period were material ones. Expansion of trade pushed for improvements in applied mathematics and arithmetic. With social pressures and changes came the proliferation of philosophical thought, with the most notable being Confucianism championed by Mencius, Taoism represented by Lao Tzu, Legalism advocated by Shang Yang, and Mohism upheld by Mozi. These schools of philosophy were and still are an integral part of Chinese civilization and way of thinking and understanding the world. Advances were also made in arts, combining both material and intellectual, from the rising importance of writings, poems, and books, to stunning artisanal work from painters and sculptors. All in all, during the Warring States Period, Chinese civilization achieved an important leap forward, surpassing in a way many, if not all, contemporary cultures.

On those bases, the first Chinese empire of the Qin Dynasty was built. With unification and establishment of a new system, Qin Shi Huangdi dealt the final blow to the feudal system, as he sought only talented people to work in his purely bureaucratic administrative system, which was solely based on laws and legality and not traditions and kinship. So, instead of giving conquered lands to his family and allies, he divided the entire empire into 36 commanderies, or provinces, which were further divided into counties. These commanderies were ruled by three high-ranking officials—civil governor, military commander, and the imperial inspector, who acted as an immediate representative of the emperor. And none of these offices were hereditary. Furthermore, the emperor realized that if his rule was going to be efficient, he had to standardize all aspects of public life, like currency, measurements, the language, and the writing system, to the details such as the width of the carriage axels. With such an organized system, the Qin empire became capable enough to exercise an impressive level of control over its population, which could be seen through large-scale public works like building roads, major canals, forts, and palaces. But this is even more obvious in the two most recognizable monuments of the ancient Chinese civilization, which are admired even today. One is, of course, the Terracotta Army, a replica of an entire army with life-sized and highly detailed soldiers, as part of the first emperor's tomb. The second one was the construction of the now world-famous Great Wall of China, as Qin Shi Huangdi ordered that the various fortifications built by states during previous periods be connected in order to protect the Qin Dynasty.

With such a powerful state government, along with a well-trained and experienced army and a booming economy, the first Chinese emperor naturally sought to expand his realm. First, in 215, he sent his general on campaigns in the north, conquering the Ordos region and parts of Inner Mongolia. With secured borders in the north, in

214, he turned his attention to the south, where he sent the majority of his armies. In a long and tough campaign against the jungle guerilla tactics of the southern tribes, his armies managed to achieve victory, pushing as far south as Hanoi, in present-day Vietnam. With those victories, Qin Shi Huang conquered and colonized large parts of the present-day provinces of Guangdong, Guangxi, and Fujian. The majority of the colonizers were actually prisoners, exiles, and poor people who were sent to assimilate the local population into Chinese civilization, to facilitate imperial rule. But despite these victories and his other administrative reforms, Qin Shi Huangdi remained rather unpopular as he was seen as a totalitarian tyrant. His punishments were cruel, and he showed little mercy. He was also criticized for murdering scholars who tried to criticize him and burned books which dealt with history and philosophies of previous eras. So, when he died in 210, not many tears were shed for him.

Commanderies (Prefectures, the Jun) of Qin Dynasty

1. Handan
2. Henei
3. Yingchuan
4. Dang
5. Xue
6. Jiaoxi
7. Linqing
8. Guangyang
9. Yunzhong

221 BC - 206 BC

19. *Map of the Qin Dynasty Chinese empire. Source:*
https://commons.wikimedia.org

And even worse for his legacy, right after his death, his ministers started plotting, putting his weaker and more pliable son on the throne, who became known as Qin Er Shi. His father's ministers used him as a puppet, worsening the regime. And as the new emperor lacked the authority of his father, rebellions quickly erupted both in the conquered lands and among the Qin armies. It soon proved that without proper leadership the Qin empire and its armies wouldn't be able to deal with the internal revolts. The second emperor tried to fight back, but his armies lost all battles, and finally in 207 suffered a crucial defeat in the heartland of the Qin state. At that time, his chancellor Zhao Gao decided he had no more use for him and forced him to commit suicide. This was the end of the Qin dynasty, state, and empire, although some sources say that Zhao Gao put Qin Er Shi's nephew on the throne, but as a mere king and not an emperor. In 206, a rebel named Liu Bang, who would become the founder of a new dynasty named Han, managed to conquer the Qin capital, capture the king, and gain prestige. But by that time, the entire Chinese state reverted to chaos with various rebel states and kingdoms proclaiming independence. There were still several years of war waiting for Liu Bang before he would manage to once again unite China.

Despite such a quick and rather undignified end of the Qin empire, it did represent the end product of the evolution of Chinese civilization during the Warring States Period. And despite all of the flaws of the short Qin imperial rule, it did create the basis of how the future Chinese empire would function, from highly developed administration and bureaucracy, through unified and standardized laws and measurements, and to the way the emperor himself would be seen and represented, through his sheer unquestionable authority. So, even though Qin Shi Huangdi was seen as a bad ruler, criticized for his lack of morality and his violent temper, many future emperors copied his bureaucratic system and parts of his royal ideology, making him and this period one of the most influential parts of Chinese history.

Chapter 5 – Rise and Fall of the Han Dynasty

With the fall of Qin came the rise of the first true imperial dynasty of ancient China. This dynasty took the best parts of their predecessors, building on their legacy to create a period that is widely considered to be one of China's golden ages. Under the Han rule, the economy continued to grow, culminating with the creation of the Silk Road that connected China with the Mediterranean. Technologies and science were also improving, with many inventions, like paper and ship rudders, becoming an essential stepping-stone for the advancement of the entire world. Of course, this newly found power of the Chinese empire was shown in military conquests that expanded the borders of China in pretty much every possible direction. It was indeed the age of prosperity and advancement in Chinese history. But to the contemporaries of the first Han emperor, it sure didn't seem like the future was going to be so bright.

As the revolts against the Qin rule multiplied, there was more than just one rebellion faction, but two stood out. One was led by the already mentioned Liu Bang, who was of a modest background serving as a local sheriff under the first imperial dynasty. The second was commanded by Xiang Yu, who was from a noble family, and who took over a rebellion in the former Chu state after the death of his uncle in battle. At first, Xiang Yu was more influential and successful, beating Qin armies in open battles and gaining prestige among other rebel forces. But to his dismay, Liu Bang beat him in the race over who would conquer the Qin capital and put an end to their dynasty. At that time, the two were still allies struggling against the old regime, but Xiang Yu grew restless and envious of Liu's success and prestige. But Liu remained loyal to Xiang, who, as the most powerful leader, was the de facto leader of the rebellion. It seems he doubted that the Qin government system was going to work in his favor, so he divided China into eighteen smaller kingdoms and distributed them. At this same time, Xiang Yu took the title of hegemon, as despite not being the first to the capital, he was still the strongest and most influential among the rebels. With that, he recreated the old system of the Spring and Autumn Period. In the division of lands, Xiang gave Liu Bang a small and remote fief called Hanzhong, in an attempt to remove him from the political stage. Of course, Liu felt betrayed and soon rose up to challenge the hegemony of Xiang Yu.

He first retook control of the old Qin state and from there started conquering neighboring kingdoms. An open conflict between the two leaders ensued. Success traded sides as neither faction could achieve a decisive victory or gain a considerable upper hand in the struggle. Eventually, both factions depleted their reserves and needed to recuperate, so in 203, Liu Bang and Xiang Yu agreed upon an armistice. A few months later in 202, Liu reopened hostilities, and this time he managed to achieve a complete victory at the battle of Gaixia, with the suicide of Xiang Yu being the most important gain. He was the only one capable enough to stand against Liu. And after his death, all the other kingdoms submitted to Liu, who was proclaimed the new emperor. According to Chinese tradition, his dynasty took the name of his home fief and became known as the Han Dynasty. Liu Bang himself became known as Emperor Gaozu.

The new ruler of this united China chose to, in most parts, follow the laws and regulations of his Qin predecessors, though he did lower the taxes and reduced military levies to both help the population recover from the civil war and to gain the loyalty of his subjects.

But Xiang's decision to divide the Qin state into eighteen kingdoms had great repercussions to the administrative system of the early Han. In the west, covering less than half of the empire, the emperor directly controlled the territory through the commanderies, emulating the Qin bureaucratic apparatus. But the eastern parts were divided into ten vassal kingdoms, all too large and led by proven generals to be conquered easily. And this fact threatened the rule of Emperor Gaozu. So, he slowly deposed of these kings, sometimes peacefully, sometimes by a show of force, giving the crowns to his family members, as he saw administrative benefits in these kingdoms. They managed to pacify the local population and ease the toll on the central government's apparatus. By 195, only one of these kingdoms wasn't ruled by a member of the Han family. Another reason why they were useful, at least when it came to the northern borders, was that they were the first line of defense against the northern tribes, who created a confederacy among them known as Xiongnu. Gaozu tried to pacify the barbarians in 200, but was defeated, and saw that the only way out was to pay tribute to them and to give the hand of a princess to their leader. Thus, he started a diplomatic practice called heqin, by using marriage as a tool to appease too powerful neighbors.

20, Emperor Gaozu of the Han Dynasty. Source:
https://commons.wikimedia.org

But even so, the first several decades of the Han Dynasty weren't stable at all. Several vassal kings rebelled after Emperor Gaozu tried to replace them, and after a battle against one of them, he died in 195, leaving a rather weak son to succeed him. At the time, the most important person in the Chinese state became Gaozu's widow, Lü Zhi, now empress dowager. As a regent of her son, she actually pulled all the strings and started giving titles, offices, and other government positions to members of her own clan. This antagonized other members of the Han family, but she remained in power until her death in 180. Under her watchful eye, three emperors changed on the throne, two of them being her grandsons, yet none proved to be able to pull away from her influence. Indeed, just before her death, one of the vassal kings from the Han family was ready to start another civil war, while the northern tribes once again raided the Chinese territories. But without her leadership, opposition to the Han kings was almost nonexistent, and their coup caused little disturbance as the Lü clan had little support. They also deposed the fourth emperor of the Han dynasty as he was seen only as the Lü clan's puppet, and the question arose who would inherit the imperial throne. Instead of looking at seniority, three Han kings chose the most suitable candidate between them, picking Liu Heng, Gaozu's son, as the most virtuous. Thus, he became Emperor Wen.

Rather quickly, it became obvious he was a good choice, as his policies were benevolent and aimed at bettering the lives of his subjects. He lowered taxes, created government aid for people in need, and made punishments for breaking the law less harsh. Under his rule, Taoist liberal teachings permeated the ideology of the central government. Emperor Wen also recognized the threat of the Xiongnu confederation, once again using the heqin policy to achieve peace on the northern borders. But he was also wise enough to realize that large kingdoms were a constant internal threat, so he used occasions when kings died without an heir to reduce the sizes of the kingdoms, without causing many revolts among his vassals. His peaceful and successful reign, which lasted until 157, was exactly what the Han Dynasty needed to stabilize their place on the throne. The effects of his reign were further expanded by the peaceful succession and rule of his son, Emperor Jing. He continued his father's policies, further cutting down on taxes and criminal punishments. He also continued his father's policy of reducing kingdoms, which finally prompted a failed rebellion of seven kingdoms in 154. After Emperor Jing's victory, the authority and power of the vassal kingdoms ensued, as well as the creation of new commanderies.

The end result of these administrative changes carried out by the two emperors can be seen in the fact that in 179 there were 19 commanderies and 11 relatively large kingdoms. By 143, there were 40 commanderies and 25 smaller kingdoms, significantly increasing the authority of the central government. Emperor Jing died in 141, leaving a stable and rather wealthy empire to his son, Emperor Wu (sometimes called Wudi). The first several years of his lengthy reign were marked by a series of reforms, as the new emperor saw flaws in the Taoist ideology and in the overdependency of the noble class, which grew strong under the rule of Wen and Jing. Despite some early opposition to his plans, Wu managed to go through with them. He reinstituted the meritocratic system in the government bureaucracy, leaving room for talented individuals of lower classes who were taught in Confucian and traditionalist thoughts. He also continued administrative changes of his predecessors, reducing the size of both the kingdoms and commanderies, thus further limiting the power of local nobles. Emperor Wu also created a position of regional inspectors, who were given a large area in which they represented the emperor and kept kings, governors, and other officials in check. This was an attempt to limit corruption and raise the efficiency of the government system.

21. Later portrait of Emperor Wu. Source: https://commons.wikimedia.org

Emperor Wu changed economic policies, abolishing the loose Taoist principles used before and adding and raising taxes. He also sought to mint money and to control mining and salt production through the state, as monopolies on those industries gave more power and wealth to the state. His government also sought to organize other parts of economic life, like trade, transportation, and prices. Wu also realized that agriculture was the main driving force of China's economy, so his government tried to stimulate it, without too many regulations, which led to the creation of a large landowner class. This was objected by some, as it led to a further rise in inequality, but he cared little about that; he needed to raise income to his treasury to fuel his campaigns and conquests. He aimed at expanding his empire in two main directions. First was to the south and southwest, conquering the Nanyue and Minyue kingdoms. This was in a way a replication of Qin campaigns, but with more permanent results, as the regions from modern-day Fujian to northern Vietnam and the eastern parts of Yenan came under the control of the Chinese empire. Roughly at the same time, Emperor Wu realized that the Xiongnu were too much of a threat, so the second direction of his campaigns was to the north and northwest.

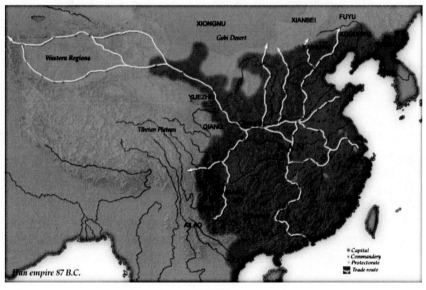

22. Han empire in 87 BCE. Source: https://commons.wikimedia.org

The Chinese armies were successful there as well, driving off the northern barbarians and expanding their territories. But due to the reports of his subordinates, who told him about the importance of trade with faraway countries which were as rich as China, Emperor Wu decided to push his conquest farther in the west, into the Gobi

Desert and Central Asia. These conquests helped the establishment of the Silk Road, a trade route which connected China with the Parthian Empire and the Mediterranean, and facilitated commerce along it. The majority of these conquests were achieved between 138 and 110, though fighting against the Xiongnu continued in later decades as well. In the ending years of the 2nd century BCE, Chinese forces also managed to conquer northern parts of the Korean Peninsula, which marked the end of Emperor Wu's expansion politics. Although he achieved vast territorial expansion, it was a rather costly venture in both human lives and money. Thus, in the later years of his reign, he focused on securing his conquests and stabilizing the internal affairs of his empire. It was clear that the burden of war fell heavy on the people, but more importantly, dynastic disputes slowly arose, culminating with the revolt of Wu's son and heir, Prince Ju, in 91/90. As a result, Wu left his throne to his youngest son, who was only 6 years old when the emperor died in 87 after ruling for 54 years, a record that wasn't broken by another Chinese emperor for another 1,800 years.

In the end, the rule of Emperor Wu was seen as a mixture of bad and good. He did raise the taxes and burden his people with long warfare, and despite his proclamations of Confucianism, he based his administrative system more on Qin legalism, ruling similarly to the first emperor. On the other hand, he did expand China into territories that to this day are part of the country, and he also furthered international trade and managed to strengthen the authority of the central government. Whether he's seen as a good or bad ruler, the fact remains that he propelled Han China to the level of a world power. But after his death came two less abled emperors, who remained under a strong influence of their regent, Huo Guang. The first of them, Wu's youngest son, died of natural causes in 74, and the other was deposed by Huo, as he was declared unfit to rule that very same year. Huo then chose Emperor Xuan for the throne, continuing to play an important role in the state until his death in 68. Those twenty odd years he was in charge he spent lowering the taxes and burdens on the people, and continued the expansion of the empire in Central Asia, but retained strict, almost despotic, rule. And as such, later historians gave him credit for being a capable administrator who acted in the best interest of the dynasty, but who overstepped his authority and ruled rather harshly.

But his death and the purging of his entire clan from the state administration in 66, changed the course of Chinese politics. Emperor Xuan further cut state spending by stopping all military campaigns and turning to diplomacy and colonization to protect the gained territories. He also refrained from an extravagant lifestyle, devoting himself to ruling as best as he could and promoting Confucianism as the state ideology. But slowly, administrative officers started to gain power, as the emperor lacked a firm hand to subdue their desires. This trend continued and even worsened after his death in 49, under the reign of his son, Emperor Yuan. Factionalism appeared among the officials, with various groups fighting for supremacy, which made the central government weaker. During Yuan's rule, some of the old kingdoms were resurrected, though for a short period, while laws became less harsh and economic control of the state lessened, though some attempts to break up lands of large landowners were made to make Chinese society more egalitarian. But in the end, that failed. And in foreign policies, he was peaceful, like his father, though some fighting occurred as the northern barbarians became restless once again. The Chinese state, together with its emperors, were growing mellow, even abandoning some of the conquered lands.

The state of the Han Dynasty worsened with Yuan's son, Cheng. He ascended to the throne in 33, and his interests lay with chasing women and enjoying life rather than ruling the empire. While he ruled, the clan Wang started to grow in power and influence in the royal court, as this was the family of Grand Empress Dowager Wang, wife of Emperor Yuan. She used her longevity and influence, exploiting the weaknesses of her son to promote her family members into vital positions in the empire. One after another, members of the Wang clan were given the high command of the entire Chinese army, and eventually, in 8 BCE, this position was given to Wang Mang. A year later, Emperor Cheng died childless, so his nephew, Ai, became the new emperor. At first, the young emperor tried to rule on his own, reducing spending, limiting slavery, and trying to force out the Wang clan from their offices. He managed to strip Wang Mang, but Grand Empress Dowager Wang was still in court, plotting. At the time, Ai got rather connected to a minor official named Dong Xian, promoting him rather quickly to higher ranks. This caused rumors of a supposed homosexual relationship, which was furthered by the fact that childless Ai wanted to leave his throne to Dong. Thus, another succession crisis emerged in 1 BCE when Ai died. Dong Xian and his entire family were forced to commit suicide, and another one of Cheng's nephews was chosen to be emperor. Wang Mang became his regent as the emperor was still a child.

23. Illustration of Emperor Ai and Dong Xian. Source:
https://commons.wikimedia.org

But the child emperor died in 6 CE, and an underage cousin related to Emperor Xuan became the emperor, once again under Wang

Mang's regency. The remaining members of the Han family were by now already irritated by the power of Wang Mang and his attitude toward them. To please them, he promised that he would relinquish all power to the young emperor when he became old enough. But in 9 CE, he dethroned him, proclaiming that the Han Dynasty lost its Mandate of Heaven, and created a new Xia Dynasty, bringing the first era of the Han to an end. By that time, Mang had full control of the royal government and forces, so he managed to quickly put down two rebellions and a mutiny that sprang up as a reaction to his usurpation of the throne. He then had to fight off raids by the Xiongnu, who once again became restless. Through war and diplomacy, he managed to once again secure peace with them by 19 CE. He also had troubles with southwestern tribes and on the Korean Peninsula, but these revolts were caused by the earlier Han reign, not himself. And once on the throne, he reformed the Chinese economy once again by monopolizing salt and iron production, monetary reforms, as well as raising old and imposing new taxes. Wang instituted an income tax for professionals and skilled laborers and a "sloth tax" for landowners if they left their field uncultivated. In essence, these economic reforms were used to once again strengthen the imperial power and gather funds to keep the government afloat.

These reforms were later seen as a sign of Wang Mang being a despotic tyrant, but in reality, he was a capable leader who ruled with great diligence, doing nothing that many emperors before him hadn't done. He even punished his own sons when they broke the law. Yet, because his attempts to start a new dynasty failed, he has been labeled as an evil emperor, and his actions were seen as the cause for his downfall. But the fact was that the Yellow River flooded twice under his rule, changing course, and causing massive famine, migrations, and general chaos in the Chinese heartland. Wang Mang tried to fix the problems, but natural disasters of that level were something that no Chinese government, not even in the 20th century, could deal with. In the end, peasant uprisings broke out in the former Qi state in 22 CE, defeating the imperial army, and then spreading farther through China. This was a perfect opportunity for the remnants of the Han Dynasty to arise, combining their forces with the peasant's, starting a full-out civil war. By the next year, Wang Mang was overwhelmed and defeated in his capital, dying in the process. The winning force proclaimed Emperor Gengshi the new leader, as he was a descendant of Emperor Jing. But he was a weak ruler not recognized by all of the rebel forces, so the civil war continued.

After a series of bad decisions, in 25 CE, Gengshi was killed, and another descendant of Emperor Jing became the new ruler of China. Emperor Guangwu was the one who actually restored the Han Dynasty. The new emperor moved his capital from Chang'an to a city called Luoyang. Because of that move, this change in the ruling branch of the Han Dynasty causes historians to divide its history into the Western Han and Eastern Han eras. But the civil war wasn't over yet. Peasants were still unsatisfied, their army roaming the Chinese heartland, and there were at least eleven other pretenders to the throne. For more than a decade, Guangwu had to fight all of them before he could confirm his position and bring much-needed peace in 36 CE. He then proceeded to rule with frugality, with the effective and efficient government once again based on capable people. He also restored the administrative division on commanderies and small kingdoms, which he gave to his family members. Guangwu also relaxed formerly strict laws, making his reign easier and more bearable for his subjects. Under his reign, he also had to deal with smaller Xiongnu raids in the northern borders as well as a rebellion in the southern regions, in what is today North Vietnam. He also waged a campaign that restored Chinese influence in Central Asia. Ruling until 57 CE, he gave the Chinese empire much-needed stability.

He was succeeded by his son, Emperor Ming. He was strict with his officials, whom he punished severely if they were reported for abuse of their power. That made the atmosphere in his imperial court rather tense, with many political plays and backstabbing among the officials. He was extremely harsh when his brothers tried to plot against him, in one case even massacring thousands of people trying to find out all the culprits. But despite that, his reign is remembered as a positive one, with many public projects that benefited economic development. Chief among them was the repair of canals, dikes, and parts of water infrastructure that was destroyed in the massive floodings of the Yellow River at the beginning of the century. In the later years of his rule, he also waged war against some Xiongnu tribes to reaffirm China's sovereignty of the Central Asian vassal kingdoms. He died in 75 CE, succeeded peacefully by his son, Emperor Zhang. He continued in his father's footsteps, working diligently and living thriftily. He sought honest and hardworking men to appoint to his government and tried to expand trade, making it easier by developing new trade routes. And like his father, he tried to stay humble by following the Confucian teachings until his death in 88. Their reigns are often considered the second golden age of the Han Dynasty, marked by a rise in prosperity, technological advances, and overall peace.

24. A tomb mural of Chinese chariots and cavalry. Source:
https://commons.wikimedia.org

One of the reasons for this kind of stability was the ability of the first three Eastern Han emperors to keep their courts relatively free of intrigue, limiting the meddling of their wives' clans, other influential officials, and eunuchs, whose role in court life started to rise. But with the new emperor, He, being a child, the empire started to revert back to the state of the late Western Han Dynasty. The Dou clan of his mother held a tight grip on the court, but thanks to his brother, Prince Xiao, and one of the eunuchs from the court, he managed to topple them and continue his rule on his own, while also relying on the advice of capable officials around him, as he lacked the capabilities of his father and grandfather. But he did provide relief in times of crisis and tried to govern as a righteous ruler. During his time, China lost control over Central Asia and had to put up with some minor rebellions in the southwestern regions. He died in 106 without a proper heir, so after some court intrigues, Prince Xiao's son inherited the throne as Emperor An. He was also only a child, so another empress dowager ruled as his regent, promoting her own Dang clanmates into vital government positions. This changed in 121 with the death of the empress dowager.

With the help of his wife, Empress Yan, and some eunuchs deposed by the Dang clan, the vacuum in power was filled by the Yan clan and the eunuchs themselves. Under An's rule, the rebellion of the Qiang people in the southwest worsened, causing further stress in the imperial budget that had already suffered depletion dealing with the natural disasters that struck China under his rule. In 124, he died, without managing to prove any worth as an emperor. Once again, a succession crisis struck imperial China, as Empress Yan tried to instate a younger prince as a ruler to exert more power in future years, but was opposed by eunuchs who themselves sought influence over the new emperor. After a series of struggles and one short rule of Emperor Shao, the empress and her clan lost the struggle. They were slaughtered, with the exception of the empress herself, and in 125, Emperor Shun came to the throne. But nothing important changed in the imperial court, as Shun was also shown to have no strength or authority, relying on corrupt eunuchs to rule.

Despite that, his reign managed to pass without too much turmoil, mostly due to his kind nature and careful choice of the empress to avoid further treachery in court. Regardless, the government was becoming ever more corrupt on all levels, making his rule less effective. However, the central imperial government under Emperor Shun worked on many local projects and once again supported the development of education and science, as seen in his restoration of the Imperial University, which had decayed over the decades. His rule is also notable for the first use of a seismograph in history, an instrument which helps detect earthquakes. And during this period, Chinese generals were also able for a short period to restore imperial influence in Central Asia, but by that time, it was clear that the power of the empire was slowly fading. Emperor Shun died in 144, leaving his one-year-old son on the throne, but he died the very next year. And here, once again, an empress dowager started exerting great influence, despite Shun's attempts to stop that. She chose another underaged heir, a great-grandson of Emperor Zhang, who was poisoned in 146 by the empress dowager's brother, Liang Ji. Next to be chosen as emperor was another great-grandson of Emperor Zhang, Emperor Huan. In the early years of his rule, Liang Ji's influence in the court grew, becoming more powerful than his sister. But Huan wasn't eager to remain their puppet, so he turned to another evil for help, to the ever-stronger court eunuchs.

In 159, they managed to stage a coup, and the Liang clan was slaughtered and all their supporters in the government purged. People expected that the situation in the empire would change, but because Emperor Huan had to rely on eunuchs to achieve this, he rewarded them with government positions, money, and power. Thus, his rule remained overshadowed by others. But he himself was a corrupt ruler, who disregarded all criticism and advice of his capable administrators, which worsened the situation. This was reflected in the numerous peasant revolts across the Chinese empire, as well as the renewed rebellion of the Qiang people in the southwest. Quelling these drained the imperial treasury, and in 161, Huan set a disastrous precedent of selling minor government positions and offices for money. Seeing how eunuchs became too powerful, several Confucian scholars that served in the central government, supported by the students of the Imperial University, tried to suppress their influence. This evolved into an open student protest in 166, which angered the emperor. He imprisoned many of them, thus turning scholars to another opposition to the throne and further alienating the people the empire needed the most, capable and educated ones. The rule of Emperor Huan ended in 168, and he died without a son.

Once again, a crucial role was played an empress dowager, Dou, who picked another child emperor descended from one of Emperor Zhao's sons. He was called Ling, and like his predecessors, he was controlled by the empress dowager's regency. Dou tried to limit the power of the eunuchs, but in the end, it backfired on her. In 169, they seized her, slaughtered her clan, and took over control of the emperor. The corruption and selling of offices and titles continued, while the eunuchs continued to plot and gain more power in the court. Taxes were raised as the imperial treasury began to dry out due to the corrupt bureaucracy. On top of all that, the Chinese army suffered a terrible defeat in 177 from the Xianbei, a new barbarian confederation in the north. All this led to a peasant revolt in central China in 184 known as the Yellow Turban Rebellion, led by a Taoist preacher who claimed that the era of the Han Dynasty was over. Despite its religious background, it was an organized attempt to seize the throne, and the central government had to send several armies to quell it. In the end, its leader was killed, and it slowly started to disband. Yet agrarian revolts, rebellions, and other uprisings continued as the state of the empire continued to decay.

The Yellow Turban Rebellion managed to cause substantial unrest, but its more important result was that for the first time generals didn't disband their armies after the imperial victory, as they sensed they would need it again soon. The rebellion also caused some court officials to persuade Emperor Ling that imperial inspectors didn't have enough power. Thus, in 188, he gave them the authority to command imperial troops and raise taxes in their regions, changing their titles to governors. Many high-ranking officials and generals were granted this new title and power, enabling them in just a few years to grow into local warlords. The very next year Liang died. His older son became the new emperor, but court intrigues continued, and after less than two weeks, he was deposed and soon after killed. Liang's other son became the next and last Han emperor. The very beginning of his rule was filled with the usual court games of the eunuchs, but this time they bit off more than they could chew, as their treachery was discovered by one of the high-ranking officers. After some political machinations, he attacked them and then executed them in 189. With that, any remaining power of the central imperial government was lost, and warlords started to arise.

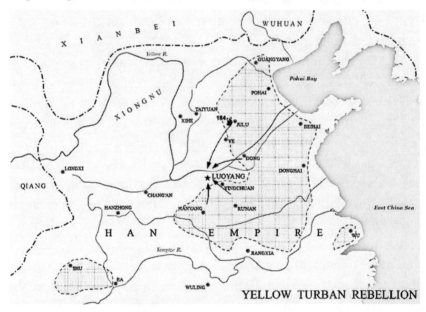

25. *Map showing the extent of the Yellow Turban Rebellion. Source: https://commons.wikimedia.org*

One of them, Dong Zhuo, seized this opportunity and took control of the emperor and the central government, calling himself chancellor of the state. Soon other warlords rose up against him, followed by peasant uprisings. This weakened his position, and in 192, he was assassinated in a court plot. After his death, most people hoped that the Han regime would return to its normal state, but the inertia of the civil war forced warlords to continue their fights as they feared retribution. Thus, the warfare continued while the imperial court lost not only its power but its source of income, with members of the central government literally dying from hunger. Emperor Xian couldn't find anyone to help him until 196 when a warlord named Cao Cao invited the emperor and his court to him. Until this period, he was only a minor warlord, but he recognized the benefits of having control of the emperor, despite his total lack of authority. He quickly gained influence, becoming one of the more important warlords in a matter of years by conquering smaller states around him. By the end of the 2nd century, China was divided into many smaller and larger warlord states, locked in all-out civil war.

26. *Last Han Dynasty emperor Xian on the left and warlord Cao Cao on the right. Source: https://commons.wikimedia.org*

At first, Cao Cao preserved the emperor's central government as it was, with all its ministers and officials. But in 208, he abolished all imperial offices, replacing them with only two, the imperial secretary and the chancellor, a title he took for himself. With that, the imperial authority of Emperor Xian was destroyed, and he became a mere puppet, similar to the earlier Zhou kings during the Spring and Autumn Period. In those early years of the 3rd century, beside Cao Cao in the north, two more warlords rose to the top, making it, in essence, a three-way fight for the throne. One was Liu Bei in the southwest, a possible distant member of a Han family, and Sun Quan in the southeast. By 220, Cao Cao died, and he was succeeded by his son Cao Pi, who shared the ambitions of his father. By the end of that very same year, he managed to force Emperor Xian to abdicate in his favor, as Cao Pi wanted to prove his power. With that act, the Han Dynasty ended after ruling China for more than 400 years. Xian wasn't killed; instead, he continued to live a rather luxurious life as a duke on a fief given to him by Pi. The other two warlords didn't wait long to raise their titles as well. Liu Bei took the title of an emperor in 221, while Sun Quan followed them both taking the same title in 229. Thus, China was divided into three states, Wei, Shu, and Wu, and the period of the Three Kingdoms began.

But despite this rather inglorious end, the Han Dynasty has been widely regarded as one of the golden ages of China. And rightfully so. Looking just on the surface, China vastly expanded its territory, from Korea to Vietnam and far into Central Asia, all the way up to present-day Kazakhstan. The economy also blossomed, both from the rise in the production of silk, iron, and ceramics, as well as because of trade. One of their most important contributions was the Silk Road that connected China to Europe. But under the Han Dynasty, Chinese culture also developed from many important philosophers and books that are still preserved today. But also, it was a period of numerous technological and scientific breakthroughs as well as developments of art. Thus, this period became a classical period of Chinese history, rather influential and regarded in ensuing generations of Chinese thinkers. And so, it was the Han who actually molded traditions of previous dynasties with their own unique attributions to create a basis of quintessential features of Chinese civilization.

Chapter 6 – Society of Ancient China

China went through enormous changes in every aspect of life during ancient times. From the time of early Shang to the late Han, China's social order, economy, bureaucracy, and even the everyday life developed, modified, and transformed. The society of the Shang is vastly different from the society of the Han, yet in this chapter, we shall try to explain some of the basic trends, characteristics, and evolution of the ancient Chinese society, but focusing more on the later Han Dynasty, as it was the period of its most complex state covered by this guide.

On top of the Chinese social hierarchy was its sovereign, and that stayed the same from the earliest days of Chinese civilization until the end of the Han Dynasty. But their titles, importance, and authority did change. The earliest historical sovereigns, not including mythical emperors, carried the titles of kings (wang), and like in most primitive early societies their rule was based on dual authority. One was their religious role, as during the Shang Dynasty and even in the early Zhou, they were vital for carrying out various rituals and ceremonies. The other was their material power, seen through simple wealth and the ability to command human resources of the commoners, both for war and for building projects. But over time, their authority grew until they were able to exert a much higher level of control over their subjects, who grew in numbers. Thus, during the Zhou Dynasty, they started to abandon their religious roles, leaving them to the priests, and focused more on developing their political and governmental functions. But during the later Zhou period, their actual authority had diminished, and they became rather insignificant. But as their nominally subordinated dukes became kings as well during the Warring States Period, their different philosophies of rule caused a change in the role of the sovereign.

Rulers of that period realized that they needed to further their own prerogatives and share less of their power with the nobles, increasing their authority. Thus, when the king of Qin became the first emperor, he took for himself absolute power. He was the only one who could issue and modify laws, as he was the supreme judge and commander-in-chief. No one could dispute his decisions, and he had the power to interfere with anyone's life. And with few exceptions, all the lands belonged to him. His ceremonial roles were almost all gone, yet there still remained a religious link between imperial authority and religion, and this was the idea of the Mandate of Heaven. First introduced by the Zhou kings, it gave the Chinese sovereigns theological legitimacy, as their authority was given and confirmed by heaven. This was especially important in periods of dynastic change, as in theory, it gave everyone the right to rebel against the emperor if his rule showed great signs of misfortune. But at the same time, it made imperial rule mostly unquestionable, making any revolts counter to the natural order of the universe. And in a way, the emperor himself equaled the state. But this dominating role of Chinese emperors was theoretical, as we have seen that their authority was often usurped by others when persons on the throne were weak.

Of course, none of the sovereigns, no matter their titles, could rule on their own. They had their officials and administrations beneath them. In the early days, the court was filled with feudal nobles, who had their own land and rights to do as they please with them. They only served the king by paying tributes and waging wars when asked. Other than that, royal authority exerted little power in the feudal states. To combat that over the centuries, the Chinese sovereigns worked on revoking feudal titles, creating a bureaucratic government. This process was finalized with the establishment of the empire in 221 BCE, but the Han Dynasty introduced an exception. Semi-autonomous fiefs were reestablished but only for members of the royal family, and their power was constantly kept in check. This, in turn, meant that pretty much all nobles were in some way connected with the imperial family. Of course, this didn't mean that other noble families disappeared. They transformed into a new class of educated gentry that served in the imperial administration. The core of the central government were positions of three excellences, whose exact titles vary. But they were the emperor's closest advisors, whose jurisdictions were separated in three often not strictly divided areas of government. Below them were nine ministers, each with their own distinct sectors, like a minister of finance or justice. They were responsible for carrying out the emperor's orders and taking care of everyday state bureaucracy.

27. *Han period figurine of two scholarly gentry men playing a board game.*
Source: https://commons.wikimedia.org

The greatest distinction between the nobles and officials is in the fact that noble titles were hereditary, but officials were appointed by the emperor. This made vertical social mobility in the Chinese society greater than most other ancient states. In theory, anyone capable could progress, but of course, wealthier people were at an advantage. For one, they had access to better education, and also their connections, which remained an important function in Chinese society, were greater, allowing them to advance faster and higher than commoners. Yet that division between the elites and the commoners was something that changed over time. In the early days, Chinese society was clearly divided into two main groups, the feudal elite and the peasant commoners. But as Chinese civilization grew more complex, the society went through stratification based on wealth and occupation. So, during the Han Dynasty, just below the nobles and officials were rich merchants, landowners, and industrialists, with the latter sometimes being outlawed by the nationalization of the industries. Landowners most often weren't working on their land, but rented it to tenants or hired a workforce to farm the lands for them while they lived in cities. Industrialists were people who dealt in the mining of metals, salt extraction, large-scale manufacturing, or animal breeding. They often owned compatible businesses, like iron mines and iron workshops, magnifying their profit in the process. And finally, there were itinerant merchants that traded with valuable commodities in a network of cities across China. It should be mentioned that often these three social groups mixed, as a single person could trade goods he manufactured while he owned large land parcels.

Below them were craftsman and artisans who created specialized articles like weapons, jewelry, and other more artistic products. Their status was solely dependent on their abilities in their craft. Some of them became rich and respected members of society, while others were measly workers without much class. Yet in the social hierarchy, they were seen as being above the local traders and small merchants, who were often despised by the gentry and sometimes even persecuted by the law, being forced to wear clothes that signified their status. An exception to this rule were booksellers and apothecaries which were seen as worthy professions by the scholarly gentry and which they sometimes engaged with. Then came the farmers and peasants, who worked on their lands. Farmers and peasants are often seen as a higher class than the artisans due to Confucian thought as they produced all the food that society depended on. This was also the only manual labor that was respected by the elites, as it was seen as something decent and humble. But of course, almost none of them worked on their own fields. Farmers had to work hard on their fields, many of them owning the lands they worked on. Others were simply tenant farmers, working on lands that they rented from the elite landowners. As they represented about 90% of the Chinese population, they were actually the base of the entire economy, so when natural disaster threatened them, the economy in whole was in danger. That is why the central government took great care to preserve this class. They were also important as they were the base for conscription, both for military service and for corvée labor, which is unpaid work owed by a subject to his feudal lord. Other lower classes were subject to this as well, but they were less numerous, thus less important.

A separate social group was that of retainers or clients, which started to form in large numbers during the Warring States Period. These were people without their own lands or possessions who lived at their hosts, providing labor for lodging, food, and in some cases wages. Two types of retainers could be distinguished. The lower and lesser respected were those who provided manual labor around the house and estate. Then there were those who served as bodyguards and combatants, who in later periods of the Han Dynasty grew into personal armies. The most notable and respected were those in advisory and scholarly roles. Some of the retainers who performed well for their hosts were even gifted luxurious items, which served to show how respected they could become.

28. Han ceramic figurines of servants. Source:
https://commons.wikimedia.org

Contrary to them were the slaves who were, of course, the lowest layer of Chinese society. They themselves were the property of their owners, and they could be split into two major groups, state and private slaves. The two most common ways to become a slave was through debt or as a prisoner of war. Yet it should be noted that slaves weren't a substantial part of Chinese society, making maybe 1% of the entire population. They never played a crucial role in the Chinese economy or way of life, and in some occasions during the Han rule, slavery was shortly abolished as it was seen as a rather immoral practice. Also, slaves were protected by the law, preventing their owners from murdering them, even in the case of vassal kings or other lesser nobilities. But children of slaves were born as slaves.

But beside this vertical division of the Chinese society into broad classes, there was also a form of horizontal division into clans, as family played an important role in the life of the Chinese. Of course, the core of these clans was the patrilineal nuclear family in which the father was the head of the family. During the Han Dynasty, it was rare to see generations of one family living under one roof. But they remained connected with their relatives with whom they shared a common patrilineal ancestor. Of course, the closer they were related, the stronger the bond. But it was common for clan members to look out for their fellow kinsmen, which in turn caused plenty of problems for the central government. The most common reason was that officials on all levels often promoted and helped their clan members, which caused those lineages to grow in power, and from time to time even threaten the imperial authority. It was also a fertile ground for corruption and nepotism in administration. Local clans were also often backbones of rebellions and revolts. And there was nothing that the government could do against the institution of the kin as it was rooted in Confucian traditions.

29. Two frescoes of noble Han women. Source: https://commons.wikimedia.org

Marriage itself was seen as part of this kinship system, as often marriages were arranged or influenced by the family head, not solely based on choices of the newlyweds. But matrilineal relatives were not considered members of the clan, and when the wife would enter a new family, she became part of the husband's clan, worshiping in his familial temple. However, she retained her natal surname. Monogamy was the norm in Chinese society, with exceptions being very wealthy nobles and imperial family. These men had one chief wife and then numbers of concubines, who legally and religiously had lesser rights. Tradition called for all women to obey their husbands and other male family members, and it was common for the mother of the clan leader to retain seniority. This was most obvious in the imperial court where empress dowagers often played crucial roles, having more authority than the emperors themselves. There were other cases when women managed to gain influence and were involved with jobs not traditionally considered suitable for them. But most of them were tasked with domestic duties, such as weaving clothes, cooking, and taking care of children. In rare occasions they worked in the fields alongside the male members of their families or wove silk or other more exclusive textiles for extra income. This was more common for widows. Divorce also existed but was frowned upon as immoral. Mostly this right was reserved for husbands, who could request it if the wife was disobedient, unfaithful, or infertile. Women could in some rare cases ask for a divorce if the husband's family couldn't materially provide for her.

Women also had some protection by the law. For one, they were excluded from corvée labor, and by the Han times, husbands were forbidden to physically abuse their wives. Rape was also banned, and women could sue their attackers in court. These, like most of the imperial laws, trace their origins to the earlier archaic forms based on customs and natural law, which matured by the time of the Han Dynasty. For example, Han legislation distinguished different types of murder, differentiating killing with intent from accidental murder. And the imperial law dealt with a wide array of offenses and obligations, outlining various forms of punishments. According to some sources, one of the early Han codices of law had 26,000 articles. Interestingly, incarceration wasn't common in Chinese law. Death sentences, usually by beheading, periods of forced hard labor, exile, and monetary fines were the usual punishments. And like most legal systems, the imperial Chinese judiciary system had several levels, from the county court, headed by a county magistrate, going up with the administrative levels of the government. In cases where jurisdiction overlapped, it was common that whoever arrested the criminal would be the first to judge the criminal.

But despite this level of development of the law system, trade remained mostly regulated by customs and personal agreements. It was a common practice in the Han period to have a contract, detailing the goods, amounts of money and dates, and other details. This was very important as it made trade more secure, further improving the economy. The first type of trade to develop was local trade, which grew into regional during the Zhou Dynasty. And after the creation of the empire, this evolved into domestic trade that covered the entire Chinese territory. Three types of goods were commonly sold, probably the most important of these being basic types of food—various types of millet, rice, wheat, beans, apricots, plums, peaches, chickens, pigs, beef, and many others. Then came the everyday commodities like oil lamps, various iron and bronze farming tools and weapons, clothing, eating utensils, ceramic wares, pottery, coffins, and even carts. In the same economic category as everyday commodities were consumables like liquor, dried fish, various sauces and relishes, spices, pickles, and similar products. The third major group consisted of raw materials like jade, metal ores, salt, hide, timber, and bamboo. A wide array of tradeable goods meant that the trade network was rather developed and important, not only for the economy but also the overall quality of life in ancient China.

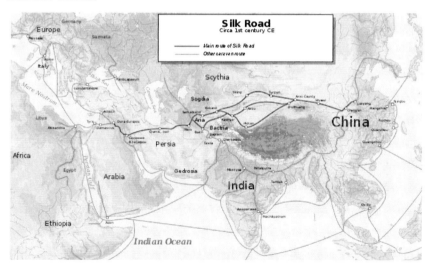

30. Silk Road route in the 1ˢᵗ century CE. Source: https://commons.wikimedia.org

But even more important than domestic trade was foreign trade, which flourished with the forming of the Silk Road in the 2nd century BCE. Before that, the main trading partners of Chinese merchants were northern barbarian tribes which offered horses and fur for food and luxurious items, most commonly silk. But with the Silk Road came more prosperous trading partners, most notably Parthians (Persians) and Romans, who themselves had rich and powerful empires. And as these were long distances, covered either by land through Central Asia to present-day Iran or by maritime routes from Vietnam across the Indian subcontinent to Persian Gulf shores, this meant the only goods traded were expensive, luxurious items. From China came silk, a highly sought after good by the Romans, but also ceramics, jade and bronze items, spices, lacquerware, and others. In turn, the Chinese imported products like gold and silver, sugar, horses, and glassware. But as the silk production was at the time a technology possessed solely by the Chinese, their economy profited more from this trade, which could in part explain the booming economy of the Han Dynasty. It is also a reminder that despite the general notion that Chinese civilization developed in an isolated bubble, it actually had connections with other nations and people around them. Though the question of direct contact between the Romans and the Chinese is still debated among historians, it is evident that the exchange of knowledge and ideas did happen.

And knowledge was seen as rather important in China, especially since the transition from feudal into a bureaucratic state system began. Gathering and sharing knowledge and experience became paramount for creating capable administrators and other officials. Thus, education started playing a rather important role in Chinese society, at least among the higher classes, which is why feudal nobles transformed into a class of scholarly gentry. There were several ways to gain an education in ancient China. There were private schools opened by teachers where they taught their students for hefty tuition fees. In some cases, rich families paid teachers to educate their heirs. From those beginnings, public education began as administration grew more complex under the imperial rule. So, on a local level, schools were sponsored by commandery governments. Most of the students attending these schools remained in local lower administration offices. More prestigious was the Imperial University in the capital, which gathered the best talents across the nation and who could only enroll based on the recommendation of higher officers. Their education was directly overseen by one of the ministers, and they were prepared for high-ranking offices in the central government. The most common topics taught were philosophy, mostly Confucianism, law, mathematics, and writing. But despite the overall importance of education for the government, it was available almost exclusively to the wealthier young males, while the poor and women were usually excluded.

From this brief introduction and description of ancient Chinese society, it should become quite clear that by the time of the Han Dynasty it became very complex. From a simple two-layered society, it grew into a system of numerous classes and vocations, with very diverse stratification. Also, clans and familial ties played an important role in pinpointing one's place in society, as well as gender. But it was a very organized and regulated system, and in many ways, it is comparable with the complexity of modern societies, with many nuances and exceptions.

Chapter 7 – The Ancient Chinese Culture

The culture of the ancient Chinese came from a very humble beginning, in a way falling behind the Egyptians, Mesopotamians, and even Hindus. But since the Shang Dynasty, it started to develop at a very quick pace and in a unique way as at the time China didn't have many connections with other civilizations. From there it became one of the most important cultures in world history, influencing much of Asia as well as the rest of the world. Thanks to that, Chinese culture is today considered by many as one of the most influential and important cultures. And it is still standing on foundations and ways of thinking set in those ancient times.

In most early civilizations, the first forms of cultural development came through religion. And in turn, religion influenced further creations in intellectual and artistic forms of culture. The Chinese were no exception in this, as shamanism and naturalistic religion were the first things that formed in the pre-dynastic times, which is today called Chinese folk religion. Their core beliefs lay in veneration of nature and balance, worshiping deities, spirits, and ancestors, as well as practicing divination and exorcism. It was based on various mythological stories and traditions, like the one retold at the beginning of this guide about the creation of the world. Exact details of these myths changed over time and also varied based on location, but a similar core remained. Beliefs were, and to some extent still are, expressed through various ceremonies, in both public and private familial temples and shrines. Yet there wasn't a unified church institution, though early kings were seen as the supreme shamans. Some of the basic concepts are the well-known yin and yang, which is the balance of light and dark, idealizing harmony and natural order. They also believed in Heaven, as seen in the Mandate of Heaven doctrine, but also in natural life, known as qi (or chi). They had numerous gods and immortals but also believed in ghosts and demons. As Chinese civilization evolved, this folk religion lost its vital importance but remained an ever-present part of everyday life of the commoners even in modern times. It also influenced later developments of philosophical thoughts in ideas of harmony or respecting ancestors and elders.

From this religious background came the golden age of Chinese philosophy in the late Spring and Autumn and early Warring States Periods. This movement became known as the Hundred Schools of Thought because of the sheer number of new schools, teachings, and philosophies. Among them, and probably the most important and influential, was Confucianism, named after its founder Confucius (551–479 BCE). It was based on idealized views of the religious traditions and values of the old Shang and Zhou Dynasties which Confucius saw missing in the chaos of his era. This is why some of the basic ideas revolved around altruism, filial piety and respecting ancestors, knowledge, integrity, and rituals. Confucian teachings state that humans are in essence good and capable of perfection, focusing on self-improvement as well as collective improvement. In essence, it was a guide on how society should work to remain in balance, as it was seen as a micro-universe, echoing the ideas of yin and yang from the folk religion. But despite having some religious aspects, like ideas of heaven or worshiping gods, it was more focused on humanistic and familial values than on the supernatural. This is why it is sometimes seen as philosophy and sometimes as a religion, especially because it left a remarkable influence on Chinese society. But maybe it would be more precise to classify it as a way of life.

31. Han period fresco of Lao Tzu and Confucius. Source: https://commons.wikimedia.org

In the same era, Taoism (or Daoism) was formulated. Its creator was semi-legendary thinker Lao Tzu (Laozi), who is traditionally considered to be roughly Confucius' contemporary. It was a more internal and religious philosophy, and as such, in later periods of Chinese history it did become a religion. Contrary to Confucianism, it was focused more on spiritual and physical growth than on political and social order. It harbored the ideas of non-violent actions, naturalness, life energy, nonaction, and relativism. It was rooted more in the metaphysical view of the universe and humans, and it preached personal growth through meditation and similar spiritual practices. Thus, it often looked more relaxed and kinder compared to strict Confucianism. But it also built upon the ideas of the folk religion and left a tremendous mark on Chinese society. And later Chinese forged a saying, "Practice Confucianism on the outside, Taoism on the inside" in an attempt to reconcile these two important worldviews.

In total opposition to these two was Legalism, another school of philosophical thought that emerged during the Warring States Period. This philosophical ideology didn't have any real founder but was a combination of ideas and thoughts of several government officials whose only concern was politics and power and who didn't care much about balance, morality, or the wellbeing of an individual. The focus of this philosophy was a regulated state, with a monarch on top that had the ultimate authority, with emphasis on the accumulation of wealth and power. The basic principle of achieving this was through severe and clear laws and harsh punishments, which is why it became known as Legalism. And where other schools of thought focused on universal harmony, Legalists were concerned with earthly order, safety, and stability. Thus, this ancient Chinese philosophy is often compared with realpolitik thought of Europeans. Besides the principle of law, Legalists also preached methods and arts of statesmanship as well as legitimacy and charisma. Another important ideal was a smaller central government, under stricter guidance of the emperor. And probably the most important ideal was the meritocratic filling of positions in the state bureaucracy. But as this philosophy heavily emphasized the power of the sovereign, it led to a more dictatorial rule, and it was far less popular after the fall of the Qin Dynasty. But it was influential in the development of the Chinese governmental system. Overlapping partially with Legalism was Mohism, founded by Mozi (470–391 BCE). It also dealt with politics and statesmanship but was seen more through impartial compassion. The only ideal these two philosophies agreed upon was the meritocratic system of government.

The core idea of this school of thought was unbiased consideration, as one should care about every person equally, regardless of their actual personal connection to the person in question. For Mohists, this was the true measure of a righteous man. Additionally, they saw society as an organized system in which inefficiency and wastefulness should be reduced, and thus promoted the idea that the moral worth of any action was measured to the extent of how much it contributed to society and the state. Another important idea was their opposition to fatalism and the role of destiny in life. Mohism thought this way of thinking brought poverty and sorrow as people refused to admit their own shortcomings and mistakes. But unlike other philosophical schools, Mohists also dealt with mathematics and engineering, mostly focused on siege and defense. And one of their sub-branches were the Logicians, who dealt with purely logical puzzles, paradoxes, and intellectual conundrums. This made Mohism important for scientific advancements and technological innovations for which the Chinese were famous, creating a precursor to the philosophy of scientific thought.

But all of these ideas and intellectual advances achieved through philosophy fade in comparison to the development of a writing system. This allowed for better communication and the sharing of thoughts, preserving them from being lost to time. The exact origins of the Chinese writing system are still unknown. The earliest verified examples come from 13th century BCE oracle bones of the Shang Dynasty, but their complexity at the time suggest writing was developed before then. However, some Neolithic archeological finds have some characters on them, and the earliest one is dated to around 6500 BCE. Though these characters and markings clearly aren't writing, some scholars did make some connections with the formation of the writing being developed in the Yellow River Basin. From the Shang period onward, it becomes far easier to follow the development of the Chinese writing system. By that stage, it had already passed the stage of a simple pictographic script, where each ideogram conveys its meaning through its pictorial resemblance to a physical object, and started to evolve into a logographic script in which an ideogram represents a word or a phrase. The next stage of writings was bronze and seal scripts, named after the most common objects and materials the writing was found on. These were dated from the Spring and Autumn Period as well as the Warring States Period. It further evolved into a logographic script with more complexity. It is worth noticing that during this period there were multiple local variations of the Chinese script. Previously, scholars thought that the next stage of script evolution, known as clerical script, developed from the seal script, but recent findings connect it with so-called vulgar, or common, writing.

32. Examples of the seal script (left) and clerical script (right). Source:

https://commons.wikimedia.org

Proto-clerical script started to emerge in the late Warring States Period in the Qin state, as it needed a simplified and faster writing system for documents and other bureaucratic needs. With the forming of a unified China, the Qin ruler standardized the writing system based upon the clerical script. This script fully matured by the early Han, and it remained the formal script of the state administration, hence the name. This is the oldest form of the Chinese script that is still partially readable today. During the Han Dynasty, the cursive style, for quicker writing, of the clerical script was formed, and it became known as the grass script. By the late Han period, a regular script, the basis for the modern-day Chinese writing system, was formed. Many other East Asian scripts evolved from that script as well, for example, Japanese, Korean, and old Vietnamese scripts. An interesting fact about the Chinese script is that, despite not being the first in history, it is the oldest script still in use today, with an unbroken line of evolution going back at least 3,500 years. But the true importance of the development of writing cannot be stressed enough. It allowed for complex ideas and thoughts to be shared, made communication easier, and helped to spread the influence of the Chinese culture to the surrounding nations and people.

Yet literacy wasn't widespread; as this writing system was rather complicated to master, it was mostly limited to the higher scholarly classes. However, members of the elite didn't use it merely for utilitarian purposes of administration and trade. They created literary works of art, composing poems and writing down stories. With most early Chinese books of poetry, it would seem that they were just folk songs, but soon original authors, like Qu Yuan (c.340–278 BCE), appeared. Poems were often allegoric and, in some way, connected with politics and morality, though in some cases they could simply describe nature or landscapes. Of course, many philosophical works were also written down, as well as histories and annals. Probably the most influential in that respect was Sima Qian (c.145-86 BCE), whose works set up the professional historiography in China and is also the prime source for most of ancient Chinese history.

Songs and poems were also connected to music, as many of them were intended to be performed accompanied by some musical instrument. Unfortunately, these tunes have been lost to time. It is known, through paintings and archeological findings, that the ancient Chinese had a variety of instruments like guqin, a string instrument of a zither type, paixiao, a bamboo pan flute, and dizi, a common bamboo flute, as well as bronze bells and drums. In the days of the Shang Dynasty, music had a ritualistic religious purpose, but in later periods, it became more focused on entertainment. However, ceremonial court music always remained important throughout Chinese history. It's also worth noting that music was often accompanied by dances, which can be divided into two major groups. One was civilian, in which dancers carried feathers and banners while dancing, and the other was a military dance with waving weapons. These also held both entertainment and ritualistic purposes.

33. Han period fresco depicting a musician and a dancer. Source:
  https://commons.wikimedia.org

Religion is also evident in ancient Chinese sculptures, as the early bronze vessels were cast primarily to be used in rituals. They had intricate zoomorphic decorations and complicated patterns but avoided human form, which became predominant in later periods. Jade sculptures and carvings also played an important role as it was one of the most popular and highly sought-after materials in China, as it was connected with health and immortality, and often used for burial objects. Even today, jade is commonly associated with Chinese culture. Of course, as time passed, the skill of the Chinese artisans grew, as did the quality of their figurines and sculptures. In later periods, clay was also used for sculpting, and the best example of this is the Terracotta Army found in the first emperor's tomb.

34. Archeological site of the Terracotta Army. Source:
https://commons.wikimedia.org

It was a collection of about 8,000 life-sized sculptures of warriors of all ranks that were supposed to accompany the deceased emperor in his afterlife. They were all sculpted with their armor on, and the features depended on their rank and unit type. All of them were armed with real bronze weapons, but most of them were looted before archeologists found the tomb. This, combined with the fact that there were also sculptures of horses and chariots, brought a high level of realism in representing the ancient Chinese army, with the final layer being bright colors that once adorned the soldiers. Unfortunately, that final finishing touch has degraded over time, leaving us today with sculptures of terracotta color. This magnificent work of art has captivated the imagination of many generations, showcasing just how capable the artists and artisans of early imperial China were. Another type of pottery, for which the Chinese are much more famous, is porcelain. It first started emerging during the Autumn and Spring Period, but true porcelain, as we know it today, was created only during the Han Dynasty. The finest pieces of porcelain were of course reserved for the emperor and the elite, complete with lavish decorations and vivid colors. At the time, they were often used as diplomatic gifts and for burial purposes, as well as for everyday use.

Paintings, on the other hand, were only used as decorations. The first decorative paintings on pottery vessels were merely patterns and shapes, but from the Warring States Period onward, the focus of artists shifted to the world around them. One example of that was frescos, painted in the tombs and temples, depicting humans in various activities. They were often scenes of triumphs or great achievements of the ruler, generals, or other prominent men. Other less permanent objects were used for painting as well, like silk or wooden folding screens. In some cases, ceramics were also painted on. And it is during the Han Dynasty that the first examples of landscapes in Chinese art were found. These types of paintings were often done by nobles, who had enough time to practice the fine brushwork needed to create these paintings. Artistic calligraphy is also connected with those. Its traces can be found during the Han period when the cursive script was formed. This skill was often highly appreciated, as it required elegance and patience, and together with painting, it was seen as the purest forms of art. Thanks to paintings, we can see other details about Chinese lifestyle, like the brightly colored silk tunics today known as hanfu. Of course, silk and high-quality furs were reserved for the nobles. Commoners usually wore clothes made out of hemp or wool.

Another major difference between commoners and the elite was the houses they lived in. Commoners' houses were often made out of mud and wood with a thatched roof. They were commonly rectangular with small inner courtyards. The village homes were sometimes connected with barns for farm animals, which were often adjacent to the main house. Floors were sometimes covered with clay or straw, and in other cases, they usually were simple dirt floors. On the other hand, nobles lived in lavish palaces and villas, commonly made out of clay bricks and stone, which were much more durable and better insulated, with decorated wooden roofs and beams. They were also rather colorful, with yellow being reserved for imperial palaces. Palaces were usually complexes of several buildings and also had inner courtyards. Contrary to most Western cultures, the Chinese put a lesser emphasis on the height of their buildings, focusing more on width to impress. This is why vaults and arches, which weren't needed as much, are not a prominent feature of their architecture, even though they existed in tombs and on city gates. Another important feature of ancient Chinese architecture was its use of expression and bilateral symmetry, signifying balance and order that is so vital to their culture. This was also seen in the grand gardens built by the elites, creating enclosed parks with forests and ponds, and adorned with flower and pavilions. First built during the Shang Dynasty, these ancient Chinese gardens attempted to express the harmony that should exist between nature and humans by crafting idealized miniature landscapes. Interestingly, most of the architectural features of the ancient Chinese civilization survived with little innovations until modern times.

35. Modern model of an ancient Chinese city. Source:
https://commons.wikimedia.org

Looking at the culture of the ancient Chinese people, two things become clear. Firstly, it evolved from a religious background, focusing more on the supernatural and deistic, developing into a civilization concerned more about humans and earthly life. Though religion and ancestral veneration never subsided, it became much less concerned with gods than Western civilizations. And secondly, it is clear that the basis of Chinese civilization founded by the end of the Han Dynasty to this day remains set in that foundation. This makes Chinese culture rather consistent, rooted in the ancient past and traditions set over 2,000 years ago. This proves the longevity and strength of the Chinese civilization, and it is why it is one of the most important in the world today.

Chapter 8 – Inventions and Innovations of the Ancient Chinese

During the period of ancient Chinese history covered in this guide, the Chinese civilization went through some significant changes, actually becoming what we associate with China today. These changes gifted the world with some of the most remarkable inventions and innovations, some being so important that they changed the world, while others show an interesting insight in how thinkers of past ages thought and solved problems. Because of this, in this chapter we'll go over some of the advancements achieved by the Chinese during this time, illuminating another part of their civilization and showing one more aspect of why it became so influential and important for world history.

36. Oldest found paper fragment from 179 BCE. Source:
https://commons.wikimedia.org

It would be only appropriate to start with probably the most important and influential invention that the ancient Chinese gave to the world—paper. Today it might not seem like such an important innovation, but it actually transformed the world by making it easier to spread the written word, thus speeding up the spread of ideas and knowledge. Before, paper rolls of bamboo strips or silk were used for writing in China. Bamboo was bulky and awkward to carry around and store, while silk was simply too expensive for common use. In the rest of the world, they used papyrus, clay tablets, or parchment for writing, but they all had similar drawbacks. But during the Han Dynasty, according to myth, a court official looking at wasps building their nest became inspired to create paper from the bark of trees, rags of cloth, fishing nets, and remnants of hemp. And according to this story, this invention happened around 105 CE. But archeological findings go as far as the 2nd century BCE, but the first use for writing on paper is evidenced in 8 BCE. It was light and cheap material, easy for everyday use. Originally, it seems it was used for wrapping and padding of bronze mirrors. Unfortunately, the

Han Dynasty didn't survive long enough to see the true explosion of paper used as a writing material, but this was still a crucial step in revolutionizing communication.

From previous chapters, it is clear that casting metal was something that the Chinese mastered early on. The earliest known cast iron was indeed found in China as far back as the 5th century BCE. But by the Han Dynasty, the Chinese refined their metal casting technology and techniques. Beforehand, they were using blast furnaces to melt iron ore in unpurified pig iron. Then they used cupola furnaces to remelt the pig iron into purified cast iron. To put this advance in perspective, modern cupola furnaces were invented in 18th century France. By 300 BCE, they discovered that through the process of decarburization, or by introducing excess amounts of air in cupola furnaces, they could produce higher quality wrought iron. It was actually wrought iron that was used for weapons and tools, making bronze finally obsolete. During the 2nd century BCE, they also realized that by combining cast and wrought iron they could create steel, a more useful and durable metal alloy. For that, they used finery forges and the so-called puddling process of stirring the molten metal with rods, both more than a thousand years before Europeans, even though steel was known since the Roman times. Their ingenuity went further as they harnessed waterpower through water-powered reciprocators to run the bellows on furnaces, reducing the need for hard manual labor in the metalmaking process.

Of course, two other inventions were needed for that technology to be implemented. The First, and arguably more important, one was the waterwheel. They weren't the first ones to invent it, as that title most likely goes to the ancient Egyptians, but the Chinese did develop it on their own, as the early waterwheel of the Han Dynasty was horizontal. Besides being used as a part of a water-powered reciprocator in the metal industry, they found their use in agriculture as well. From their use of pestle and mortar, the ancient Chinese developed water-powered trip hammers they used for thrashing, decorticating, and polishing grain. Hydraulic power was also harvested by chain pumps connected to the waterwheel, which were used to lift the water into irrigation channels. This system was also adapted to lift the water into a stoneware pipe system of the imperial palace and nobles' living quarters, creating, in essence, an ancient plumbing system. But the waterwheel wasn't the only invention needed to make a water-powered reciprocator. They also needed a belt drive, which was created during the 1st century BCE. This was a system in which belts were used to link two rotating shafts to transmit power. The first recorded use of a belt drive was in quilling devices that were used to wind silk fibers onto spools. In the reciprocator mechanism, it was used to connect the waterwheel shafts with the bellows.

Mechanical ingenuity of the ancient Chinese didn't stop there. The earliest crank handles, which were operated by hand, were discovered in China dating to the 2nd century BCE. They were used to power fans in a winnowing machine used to separate the chaff from the grain. In later periods, this technology was adapted for other uses. Ancient Chinese engineers also developed the gear as early as the 4th century BCE. They were both made out of wood, but also from cast bronze and metal. Their applications were numerous, as it transmitted harnessed waterpower to finer mechanical creations like the odometer cart, which measured covered distances thanks to a complex system of gears powered by the rotation of the wheels. Chinese inventiveness and understanding of nature can also be seen through their invention of the first seismograph that showed the direction of earthquakes. It did so thanks to a pendulum inside a bronze vessel that would swing as the earth shook, hitting a mechanism on one of the eight sides that represented major directions of the earth. The crank-and-catch mechanism would then release a metal ball that would drop and alert people nearby with its loud noise that an earthquake would happen. Their observance of nature can also be seen in their early lodestone compasses. Lodestone is simply naturally magnetized mineral, which when freely suspended point to the magnetic poles of the Earth. But these weren't used for navigation for another ten centuries; instead, they were utilized for geomancy and fortune telling.

37. *Han Dynasty era mold for a bronze gear. Source:*
https://commons.wikimedia.org

The Ancient Chinese also made several advances in medicine, despite it being firmly rooted in religious and philosophical practices, as it was connected with the ideas of life force, balance, and harmony. Chinese physicians realized that the ephedra plant, which contains ephedrine, could be used as an antiasthmatic and stimulant. They practiced dietary treatments and prescribed preventive exercises, similar to present-day Tai Chi, and it is during these ancient times that the practice of acupuncture was developed. Their physicians were keen observers, so they were able to recognize and describe symptoms of leprosy and diabetes, though they didn't have a proper cure for these illnesses.

But the physicians weren't the only ones in the Chinese society proficient in observing and noting natural occurrences. By the end of the 2nd century CE, Chinese astronomers had cataloged over 2,500 stars and 120 constellations. To represent them and to aid astronomers with the calendrical computations and calculations, they had built an armillary sphere (spherical astrolabe) during the 1st century BCE, roughly at the same time as Westerners did. But later Chinese armillary spheres were made automatized by hydraulic power. And it was the Chinese astronomers who observed the first sunspot in the mid-4th century BCE. By the time of the Han Dynasty, they theorized that light came only from the sun and that moon and planets were only reflecting that light. And like many other ancient civilizations, they knew about only five planets, Mars, Jupiter, Venus, Saturn, and Mercury, all of which are visible to the naked eye. They also believed that the sun, moon, and planets were actually spherical balls, despite still supporting the idea of a geocentric universe.

Lowering their gaze from the stars, the ancient Chinese focused on the earth beneath them. The earliest map dates from the 4th century BCE, showing the tributary river systems of the Jialing River in present-day Sichuan, along with administrative counties, roads, as well as timber gathering sites and their distances to them, being possibly the oldest economic map found so far. They also wrote books with geographical information, describing the traditional nine provinces, their characteristic goods, type of soil and agriculture systems, and even their revenues. The oldest such book dates to the 5th century BCE. During the Han Dynasty rule, cartography was further developed, and Chinese maps became more detailed and precise. Cartographers also started creating relief maps. An interesting change was made in their evolution as Qin maps placed north at the top, while Han cartographers put south on top.

Going further down into the earth below, the Chinese also pioneered new types of mining techniques called borehole drilling. The drill would be rotated by draft animals while several men jumped on top of it to create a narrow shaft that reportedly could reach depths of up to 600 m (2,000 ft). They were most often used to mine for brine, a high-concentration solution of salt in water. To extract the salt, they boiled the brine. According to some archeological findings, while they were mining for brine, they stumbled upon natural gas. By 500 BCE, they found a way to use it, transporting it from the ground in crude pipelines of bamboo, by boiling the salty water. Besides being the first to utilize natural gas by the 1st century BCE, they had also found and started to use unrefined crude oil.

But observation and practical use weren't the only scientific fields in which the ancient Chinese excelled. They also achieved several impressive mathematical breakthroughs. In the Shang era, they had already developed basic arithmetic, a decimal system, and equations. Historians aren't sure if they also adopted the idea of negative numbers at that time, but by the Han Dynasty, they surely did. So, while most of the Hellenistic and Roman world saw negative numbers as an invalid result, the Chinese saw it as a viable solution, as it represented a duality represented in their idea of yin and yang. By the end of the Han Dynasty, Chinese mathematicians had also calculated pi to 3.14 and created their own Pythagoras' Theorem known as Gougu Theorem, meaning they also understood the ideas of a square cube and square root. Besides being the first civilization to adopt the idea of negative numbers, they also left the earliest evidence of a decimal fraction in the 1st century CE. The most developed achievement of ancient Chinese mathematics was creating the Gaussian elimination (row reduction), an algorithm used to solve linear equations by the end of the 2nd century CE. This was achieved in Europe only in the early 18th century. From the mathematical textbooks written down during the Han rule, it is clear that their math first developed as a need for trade, then improved for the needs of the state, calculating taxes and surfaces of plots, as well as dividing labor and other administrative tasks. Only by the late Han, when mathematics got advanced enough, did it become more focused on solely resolving theoretical problems.

38. Model of the Warring States Period traction trebuchet. Source: https://commons.wikimedia.org

Less theoretical and more practical were the Chinese advances and inventions in military equipment. The most notable invention was, of course, the crossbow. The oldest archeological evidence of it is dated to the mid-7th century BCE. Crossbows remained the most valued weapon among the ancient Chinese. In later periods of the Warring States Period, crossbows were enlarged and mounted on wall towers, and used for both attack and defense. And the design of the crossbow itself became more sophisticated over time, with more precise and stronger mechanisms, as well as becoming lighter and easier to use. From the 5th century BCE, Chinese were also using war wagons on the battlefield, which served as a mobile armored cart to protect the soldiers. Most often it was used during sieges, to protect the archers or the tunnel diggers from the defender's projectiles. By the 4th century BCE, traction trebuchet, also known as mangonel, was created, which used manpower to hurl large pieces of stone at defenses of a city with high accuracy and rate of fire. During the Spring and Autumn Period, the first accounts of martial arts appear in military textbooks. This is a hand-to-hand combat system that includes techniques such as strikes, joint manipulation, pressure point attacks, and throws. From these early beginnings, the famous Chinese martial arts developed, becoming one of the recognizable signatures of their civilization.

Some other innovation made by the ancient Chinese could be described more as cultural than anything else, but nonetheless tied in with their civilization and influence with other cultures. Probably the most iconic and influential are chopsticks. The earliest found date to around 1200 BCE, and they were made out of bronze. But scholars think they were invented long before that, at least during the mythical Xia Dynasty, if not further back to the Neolithic times. Their use has spread across East Asia and now are irreversibly connected with our notion of Asian cuisine. Another invention connected with Chinese cooking are woks and stir-frying. There are indications of them being used in the Spring and Autumn Period, but the oldest confirmed wok dates from the Han Dynasty. It should be noted that boiling and steaming remained more popular in traditional Chinese cuisine until the late Middle Ages. Another Chinese innovation that has spread across the world is drinking tea. Chinese have been drinking tea, going as far back as the Shang Dynasty, at first as a medicinal and ritualistic drink, but later as a stimulative drink. Another food-related novelty devised by the ancient Chinese is soy paste and sauce. Created by the Chinese during the Han Dynasty, they were used as a way to stretch out the use of salt, which was rather expensive. Ancient Chinese enjoyed sports as well, one of them being cuju, a Chinese variation of football (soccer), that involved kicking a ball through a hole in a net. It was first used as a military exercise in the 3rd century BCE, but during the Han Dynasty, it became the sport of the nobles. Despite dying out later on, today it's recognized by FIFA as the earliest form of football in history.

There are many more inventions, innovations, and knowledge with which the ancient Chinese have influenced the world and its development. This just goes to show how advanced their civilization had become by the start of the imperial era, having numerous inventive men looking for ways to improve the lives of other people around them. So, it goes to show that the old Western notion of Europe being a center of technological and scientific superiority is a simple misconception created in the European colonial era. The Warring States Period, alongside with the Han Dynasty rule, was the first burst of scholarly and technological leaps made by the Chinese people, leaving inventions that are often seen as modern technology. And it once again shows why the Chinese civilization is so important and why it should be studied.

Conclusion

Looking at the history of ancient China, several things become evident. It is a civilization that was created and made its first steps in isolation, far away from other cultures. This is why many of its ideas and foundations seem so different from most others of the time. Yet, looking at how it developed, it becomes clear that no matter how different it may seem it had gone through ups and downs like any other civilization, showing that beneath the layers of culture and history lays something that connects us all—humanity. Despite how far apart civilizations grow and how unique they are, the human spirit is what moves it. And that is why Chinese history is also filled with numerous great men, generals, inventors, and philosophers, as well as conspirators, tyrants, and decadent drunks. In that aspect, ancient Chinese civilization is no exception.

But at the same time, thanks to the very unique path it took in its development, Chinese civilization and society remain strikingly different from Western cultures. And this difference is visible even today, as the root of modern Chinese culture lies in foundations set in ancient times. But different shouldn't mean worse or bad. Just by reading this short introductory guide, it should be clear that ancient

China achieved many feats. On a political scale, it managed to conquer vast areas and unite tens of millions of people under one border and government. From humble beginnings, China indeed became a strong and wealthy empire. And Chinese people managed to create stunning pieces of art, gather tremendous knowledge, and build many wondrous inventions. Its ideals were equality and welfare for all, striving for balance and harmony. Looking at all this, it becomes clear how and why ancient China is so influential. But one thing should be emphasized: these were only the first steps of Chinese civilization. It was still in its youth. In those first 2,000 years, it went through many changes and upheavals, but it prevailed. Since then, almost 2,000 more years have passed, and this culture is still going strong, slowly rising back to the top as the strongest, wealthiest, and most technologically advanced country in the world. And looking at its past, it is in its rightful place.

At the same time, learning about ancient Chinese history reminds us that human civilization didn't develop from only one center and didn't follow one simple straight line. Too often, the Western world disregards other cultures and civilizations, thinking their histories are less significant. But it is important to remember that humanity is diverse: it grew from many roots, each civilization giving something to mankind, which influenced the development of the global world civilization that we have today. One of these roots is ancient China.

In the end, hopefully this guide has piqued your interest to find out more about ancient China and Chinese civilization in general. Because knowing and appreciating our collective past is important if we want to understand each other and comprehend the present, and if we want to develop a better future together.

Short Timeline of Ancient Chinese History

c. 2070 BCE - Mythical Xia Dynasty was created

c. 1600 BCE - Rise of the Shang Dynasty

c. 1350 BCE - Anyang becomes Shang capital, start of the Shang golden age

c. 1250 BCE - Oldest remains of Chinese script found on oracle bones

1250 to 1192 BCE - Reign of greatest Shang king Wu Ding

1046 BCE - A grand battle of Muye and the start of Zhou Dynasty

957 BCE - Zhou expansion stopped by death of King Zhao

841 BCE - Revolt against the Zhou rule and exile of the King Li

771 BCE - The Zhou court moves east and the start of the Autumn and Spring Period

7th century BCE - Invention of the crossbow

667 BCE - Duke Huan of Qi becomes first hegemon

551 to 479 BCE - Life and works of Confucius

546 BCE - Jin, Chu, Qi, and Qin states arrange truce and divide spheres of influence

5th century BCE - Invention of cast iron technology

476 BCE - Beginning of the Warring States Period

470 to 391 BCE - Life and work of Mozi

458 to 403 BCE - Partition of Jin

344 BCE - Rulers of Qi and Wei become first kings outside the ruling dynasty

288 BCE - Rulers of Qi and Qin attempt to proclaim themselves emperors

269 BCE - Defeat of Qin and start of the king Zhao's reforms

247 BCE - Zhao Zheng became king of Qin

230 to 221 BCE - Final unification of China, King Zhao becomes Qin Shi Huangdi

210 BCE - Death of Qin Shi Huangdi

206 BCE - Fall of Qin Dynasty

202 BCE - Liu Bang becomes Emperor Gaozu and starts the Han Dynasty

2nd century BCE - Invention of paper

180 to 157 BCE - Reforms and rule of Emperor Wen

145 to 86 BCE - Life and work Sima Qian, establishing Chinese historiography

141 to 87 BCE - Conquests and expansion of China under rule of Emperor Wu

9 CE - Wang Mang's coup and attempt to establish a new dynasty

22 CE - Peasant uprising in former state of Qin

25 CE - Restoration of the Han Dynasty and moving of the capital to the east

57 to 88 CE - Rules of emperors Ming and Zhang, golden age of the Han Dynasty

125 to 144 CE - Development of education and science under Emperor Shun

161 CE - Emperor Huan starts selling administrative offices, weakening and corrupting the government

184 CE - The Yellow Turban Rebellion begins, led by a Taoist preacher

189 to 220 CE - Reign of the Emperor Xian and the fall of Han Dynasty

Here are some other books by Captivating History that we think you would find interesting

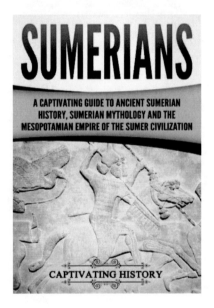

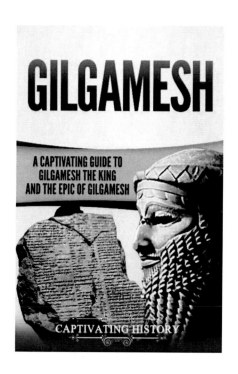

THE ROMAN EMPIRE

A CAPTIVATING GUIDE TO THE RISE AND FALL OF THE ROMAN EMPIRE INCLUDING STORIES OF ROMAN EMPERORS SUCH AS AUGUSTUS OCTAVIAN, TRAJAN, AND CLAUDIUS

CAPTIVATING HISTORY

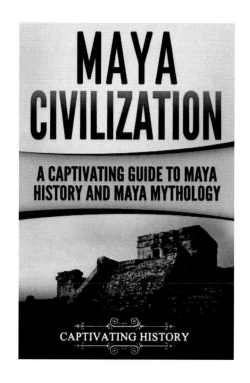

CAPTIVATING HISTORY

Bibliography

Chey O.S., *China Condensed: 5000 Years of History and Culture*, Marshall Cavendish Editions 2008.

Clunas Craig, *Art in China*, Oxford University Press 1997.

Dawei C. and Yanjing S., *China's History*, Cengage Learning 2011.

Ebrey Patricia B., *Chinese Civilization: A Sourcebook*, The free press 1993.

Fairbank J.F. and Goldman M., *China: A New History*, Harvard university press 2006.

Gernet Jacques, *A History of Chinese Civilization*, Cambridge University Press 1996.

Giles H.A., *Religions of Ancient China*, Blackmask Online 2000.

Greenberger Robert, *The Technology of Ancient China*. Rosen Publishing Group 2006.

Hinsch, Bret, *Women in Imperial China*, Rowman & Littlefield Publishers 2002.

Keay John, *China: A History*, Harper Press 2009.

Keightley D.N., *Origins of Chinese Civilization*, University of California press 1993.

Kinney A.B. and Hardy G., *The Establishment of the Han Empire and Imperial China*, Greenwood Press 2005.

Loewe M. and Shaughnessy E.L., *The Cambridge History of Ancient China*, Cambridge University Press 1999.

Morton W.S. and Lewis C.M., *China: Its History and Culture*, McGraw-Hill 2005.

Pletcher Kenneth, *The History of China*, Britannica Educational Publishing 2011.

Twitchett D. and Fairbank J.F., *The Cambridge History of China: Vol. 1*, Cambridge University Press 1986.

Watson W., *The Arts of China to AD 1900,* Yale University Press 1995.

Xueqin L., *Eastern Zhou and Qin Civilizations*, Yale University Press 1985.

Free Bonus from Captivating History (Available for a Limited time)

Hi History Lovers!

Now you have a chance to join our exclusive history list so you can get your first history ebook for free as well as discounts and a potential to get more history books for free! Simply visit the link below to join.

Captivatinghistory.com/ebook

Also, make sure to follow us on Facebook, Twitter and Youtube by searching for Captivating History.

Made in United States
North Haven, CT
06 December 2023

45116793R10081